BORN, NOT RAISED

Take care of your kids cause
it sucks when no one cares.

Yale (boy), age 15

BORN, NOT RAISED
VOICES FROM JUVENILE HALL

SUSAN MADDEN LANKFORD

HUMANE EXPOSURE PUBLISHING, LLC

san diego, california

For my daughter Polly

HUMANᴇ EXPOSURES PUBLISHING, LLC

EDITORIAL
Susan Madden Lankford, Lydia Bird, Anne Marie Welsh

DESIGN
Susan Madden Lankford, Polly Lankford-Smith, Anton Khodakovsk

PHOTOGRAPHY
Susan Madden Lankford, Polly Lankford-Smith

Library of Congress Control Number: 2011937984

Lankford, Susan Madden
Born, Not Raised: Voices from Juvenile Hall

ISBN-13: 978-0-9792366-3-1
ISBN-10: 0-9792366-3-0

Usage Rights:
Photograph of Albert Einstein, page 23 & 129, photo by Philippe Halsman / © Halsman Archive
"Head On" c. 1920, page 33 & 35 - All Rights Reserved
Photograph of Gertrude Stein, page 21, © Estate of Horst P. Horst / Art + Commerce
Photographs of former Angola Prison Death Row Inmates,
page 133 & 150, photos by John Ramsey Miller / © John Ramsey Miller
Drawn timeline, initial design by Diane Campbell, M.D.

The names of the youths have been changed to
protect their confidentiality.

Criminal Justice / Juvenile Justice / Social Justice / San Diego (Calif.)

This book was produced in a socially and environmentally responsible manner.

Cover Design: Anton Khodakovsky and Humane Exposures

Printed in China through Global PSD

Every child is born innocent.

This is the house of a very sick
person. He is a cereal dog murderer.
He has several Male dog heads
lined up in his back yard, One
of them he cut into thirds
and put it on this brick wall.

Contents

It look like A boy who is Playing with his dad. That lucky motherfucker. SHit I don't got A dad. That motherfucker left me a long time a go. that why I do what I do today.

Seda (boy), age 15

Foreword

With all thy getting, get thee understanding.

—**Proverbs**

In this closing volume of her piercing trilogy on the realities of human development underlying three dramatic forms of failed lives, photojournalist Susan Madden Lankford, again working as an urban anthropologist, takes us with camera and tape recorder to the beginning of it all, what others don't want to see: life experiences in childhood, illustrated by the lives of the children in San Diego's Juvenile Hall. The very title of this book is our beginning insight into the major role of failed or absent parenting. We are readily reminded of T.S. Eliot's quote, "In my beginning is my end."

Susan Lankford shows us in her photographs and recorded conversations from Juvenile Hall how early teen pregnancy, drug use, violence, and gang membership are the markers for far more serious, uncomfortable, and pervasive social issues. They are much like the smoke that indicates a house fire: obvious, sometimes lethal, but not the essence of the problem. The problem with mistaking the byproduct for the cause is that it leads to well-intended but ineffective solutions. Currently the United States has the highest percentage of its population in prison of any developed nation, and its lead is increasing. Might we be missing some basic point?

Born, Not Raised breaks through social taboos against exploring the family origins of delinquent juvenile behavior. Who ever read in the media anything insightful about the families who created the Columbine shooters? The objective evidence Mrs. Lankford presents is interspersed with excerpts from interpretive conversations between her, her daughter, Polly Lankford Smith, and psychiatrist Diane Campbell. Dr. Campbell helps us understand not only what is going on, but why.

This is an important book, and surely not a comfortable book. It clearly illustrates the vast gap between what we believe of ourselves as a successful society, and the dark side that contains our failures, which we prefer to lock up and overlook. We repeatedly see that in addition to their manifest problem behaviors, many of the adolescent Juvenile Hall inmates are incapable even of coherently expressing their powerful thoughts and feelings in writing, and the reasons underlying that inability. The personal as well as the economic implications of this are enormous.

Ultimately we realize that any book about the human condition is a book about relationships. This unusual book, like its two predecessors, is built from the author's carefully documented relationships with this third category of society's untouchables. There is much to be learned in *Born, Not Raised*: about the major social problem of children in the juvenile justice system, about human development and our profound need for attachment to stable caregivers during the early years, and about ourselves. This book is an important starting point, the closest the rest of us will ever come to seeing and understanding what underlies the interpersonal, social, economic, and health failures in the lives of these young citizens.

—Vincent J. Felitti, M.D.

Kaiser Permanente Medical Care Program
Clinical Professor of Medicine, University of California, San Diego

How did these kids get into this mess?

Has society lost interest in these youths
because we can't find easy solutions
for stopping the crimes that lock them up?

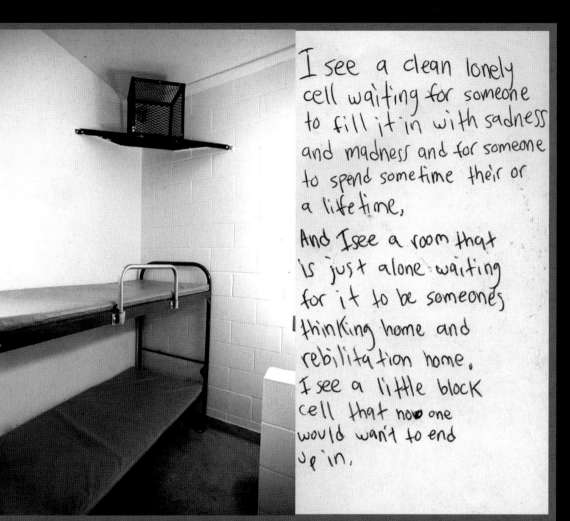

I see a clean lonely
cell waiting for someone
to fill it in with sadness
and madness and for someone
to spend sometime their or
a lifetime,

And I see a room that
is just alone waiting
for it to be someones
thinking home and
rebilitation home.
I see a little block
cell that now one
would want to end
up in.

Martinez (boy), age 15

I see a bathroom in a jail cell. I see no freedom, no privacy, no life. I see a place of confinement, a place of punishment, a place with no happiness. I see me!

Could the answer
lie in parenting, education,
and learning to raise our children
responsibly in today's world?

Kearny Mesa Juvenile Detention Facility – San Diego, CA

Introduction

I had been interested in what goes on in Juvenile Hall for many years, long before I tackled two photojournalism projects—the first about San Diego's homeless population and the second about incarcerated women. The latter spurred me on to Juvenile Hall as a natural consequence of meeting so many incarcerated women with children in the criminal justice system—supervised by either dependency courts, which remove children from their families and place them with relatives or foster parents, or delinquency courts, which determine placement for youths who have broken the law.

I also have three daughters. In any U.S. family with teens in high school today, there is a high probability that a classmate of one of our own children will end up in Juvenile Hall.

My daughter Stacey was in a physics class with a young fellow who was sent to the Hall. Stacey was shocked. "What's that place like?" she asked. We drove to the Hall, but were unable to enter, so we tried to imagine what it was like inside. Her fellow physics student, Alex Valentine, was released, and later—after flunking out of the prestigious Harvey Mudd College—returned home, and murdered both of his parents. He is serving a life sentence.

During that time period, teens from the same high school were involved in a terrible accident. Out of control on alcohol and pot, the foursome left an unchaperoned party and drag raced with other teens, their car ending up wrapped around a eucalyptus tree in front of our home. I heard the cries of the young people at midnight. My husband and I rushed to the shouts of "Help!" after calling 911. It took more than the Golden Hour to extricate all the injured bodies. One of the teenagers did not survive.

I was overwhelmed by the fatality and its tragic impact upon our community. I had felt the same intense emotions when I discovered that Alex Valentine, a very bright young man, had been severely troubled and obviously not helped. It was apparent to me that we, as parents, must find answers. If a youngster loses his or her essential footing within the family, bonds are broken, and parents are responsible for what happens.

My first experience with a jail setting came when I left a successful photography career and tackled a new photojournalistic approach, initially renting an unused jail in downtown San Diego as the backdrop for commercial photography. Homeless people hung around the old jail and asked me what I was doing. A couple of regulars talked me into touring the streets with them. Soon I was making new discoveries, learning more about our society by seeing its underbelly. By letting me photograph and tape-record their tales and journeys, the homeless showed me the darker side of downtown life.

Suddenly I was doing real-life portraiture of very expressive and open individuals. I discovered that all of them had served many stints inside our local jails. This made me wonder how street people deal with total confinement. And, how much did this cost? What did the homeless gain from incarceration? Or did they simply land back on the streets? How many homeless people were in our jails? I had always imagined that our jails and prisons were full of serious, probably dangerous felons.

My project with the homeless led me into a women's detention facility where I discovered that many of the inmates had children in foster care or in Juvenile Hall. As with these previous projects, I had to clear several hurdles before getting approval for me and my daughter Polly, then a university senior majoring in art and psychology, to enter Juvenile Hall and work with the incarcerated young people. Our goal was to find out how these youths ended up in this mess, as well as to see how we as a society deal with locking them up.

The cycles in the lives of society's disenfranchised—on and off drugs, in and out of jail, on and off the streets—were all too apparent. Abuse and neglect were the toxins that poisoned these lives and directed them into unsuccessful patterns.

Juvenile Hall was clearly the next step in my journey of research and discovery.

San Diego Hall of Justice – San Diego, CA

1

Getting In
Not That Easy

> We said there warn't no home like a raft, after all. Other places do seem so
> cramped up and smothery, but a raft don't. You feel mighty free
> and easy and comfortable on a raft.

—**Mark Twain**, *The Adventures of Huckleberry Finn*

When I decided to tackle the next portion of my criminal justice study and request access to Juvenile Hall, I first met with Judge James R. Milliken, the Presiding Judge of the Juvenile Court, to get my bearings. I had met Judge Milliken earlier, before I ever entered Las Colinas Jail, the women's detention facility that was the foundation of my book about women doing time. He was then serving on the Superior Court and explained what permissions I would need to enter that jail; he now told me that to enter Juvenile Hall I would need to go through the Department of Probation. The County of San Diego Sheriff controls entry to adult detention facilities such as Las Colinas; the Chief of Probation controls entry to Juvenile Hall facilities.

Henry Shankman, the Probation Officer for youths-at-risk in Oceanside, a suburb of San Diego and one of the toughest jurisdictions for delinquency issues, was my first stop. Our meeting was short and sweet.

Shankman summed up the conditions that lead young people into Juvenile Hall. "You're talking child abuse, you're talking detox babies, you're talking homes that look like they've been run over by a car and the family's still living there," he said. "Homelessness, problems in school, foster care, a lot of kids not in foster care who should be, kids getting into shoplifting, sex play that gets out of hand, wanting to steal cars—all contribute to what keeps us busy in Probation."

My next stop was a meeting with Al Crogan, Chief of the San Diego Department of Probation. Crogan provided his own list of the most common reasons that youths end up in the criminal justice system:

1. Leaderless family
2. Expulsion from school or truancy
3. Substance abuse (not experimentation)
4. Theft
5. Runaway status

Crogan agreed to my request to talk to these youths and ask what route they took to get where they are. But I also needed approval from Frank Bardsley, the County Public Defender. During our meeting, I learned a great deal from Bardsley, especially about gangs, guns, and drugs and their relationship to violent juvenile crime.

> **Bardsley**: If a juvenile is charged with a serious crime and tried as an adult, he's no longer Johnny J. All those protections fall away. In the juvenile court, everything remains in a pretty closed setting with inaccessible records.

When you see some 13- or 14-year-old sitting on a telephone book in the courtroom because he's so small, unable to comprehend what's going on, being judged by a panel of 50-year-olds, it's real dramatic...

Susan: Jim Milliken said to me that the only hope is with the youths. Do you agree?

Bardsley: I never met a 14-year-old and said you can throw this kid away at this age with no hope. What is the decision-making ability of any teenager? We just can't say that at age 14 or 15 you're finished for all your life—70 years. You'll die in prison. I wonder if people really understand. My message is that I don't think the answer lies in the courts at all. The courts are a necessary evil. Once the kids get into the courts, we've lost them.

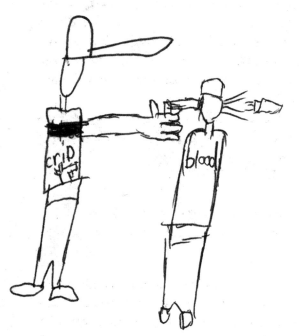

Seda (boy), age 15

The courts begin and end with Juvenile Court, and if that's not done effectively we'll end up with more and more people in more and more prisons.

Susan: How much youth crime comes from the gang element?

Bardsley: A lot of it, but gangs aren't as important in my view as guns and drugs. Getting into social groups has gone on for decades. When I was growing up in the Midwest in the '40s and '50s—you'll understand this—kids in Iowa who didn't have anything better to do got together in gangs, but they didn't have guns and drugs. They could effect a punch in the nose but not a blow to the brain. If we could get guns out of society, people would be a lot less concerned about gangs.

We have enough handguns in this country to arm everyone two or three times over.

For drugs, you need money. It's not so much they blow their brains out—they do that, too—but we're talking big money, and guns in the hands of kids who've seen 200,000 homicides on TV by the time they're 12 years old, who have no concept of what they're doing or what it all means.

I worked for the public defender's office in L.A. for almost 20 years, and a good part of that time I was trying nothing but murder cases. When I started supervising the downtown felony lawyers, I read every homicide case in the central district of L.A. and assigned the lawyers. I couldn't drive anyplace from downtown L.A. to the ocean without pointing out crime scenes to my wife—a homicide occurred on that corner, that alley is all guns. People are dying in that community all over the place because of the guns.

Susan: What percentage of the crime was gang-related homicide?

Bardsley: I think most of those kids are in some sort of loose association with a gang. Was it a homicide because of a gang, or did the person who committed a homicide just happen to be in a gang? To grow up in Watts, Compton, Southeast L.A., or the equivalent areas in San Diego and not be in a gang is tantamount to riding around with a death sentence. All the kids are in gangs. They almost have to be.

Bardsley gave me an overview of how the juvenile justice system functions. He surprised me with his optimism. He said that the book I planned to create, as long as each youth remained unidentified, could be a hopeful tool to help families comprehend the gravity of the situation faced by our young people today. He even suggested, passionately, that I go into the courtroom during sentencing to photograph a young teen from the back, to reveal through body language that the child was in shock and had no comprehension of the crime he'd committed.

> Gangs aren't as important in my view as guns and drugs.
>
> —**Frank Bardsley**, *former County Public Defender*

He said Bill Boyland and Beth Shoesmith—public defenders who worked directly with the youths, managing their care in the hands of probation—could shed more light on the situation of these kids.

I met with Bill Boyland for lunch. Just as Bardsley had suggested, he was open, caring, and very willing to share his knowledge. He also seemed saddened, even desperate, that things were getting worse, not better.

When his boss Frank Bardsley sent him to work in the juvenile system, he said, "We'd both been practicing criminal law all our lives and we both know that people in the adult system today were in the delinquency system yesterday and the dependency system the day before that. Now our job is to straighten them out as dependents and as delinquents, so we can stop this thing."

I soon learned the difference between dependency court and delinquency court. Dependency court removes children from their families and places them into foster care or with another relative. Delinquency court determines placement for youths who have broken the law.

> **Susan**: You accepted that job.
>
> **Boyland**: It's called realistic idealism. It's a peculiar thing. We work with the dependency system and the delinquency system. We're the only ones who see it close up and understand its progression. Other people see it in pieces.

Boyland further described the two different aspects of the criminal justice system for children and teens. Delinquent youths are those who have committed a crime and are in the hands of probation—sometimes probation while living at home, sometimes more serious levels of incarceration. Dependent youths are in the hands of social services, and are typically placed into foster care or with a relative.

> **Boyland**: I understand the criminal justice system and carry either the baggage or the badge of having been a judge and then a mayor. The cases are so stressful that the stress saps the strength of people who work with these kids. Especially women. They worry all night about their cases. They don't sleep. They get autoimmune diseases and become disabled. Women are drawn to this work because the;re's a whole lot of mothering to do. You're dealing with little kids. Even if they're charged with using machine guns to kill other kids, they're still little kids.
>
> **Susan**: I can't get a nice tidy picture... The child has a gun, his mother is on drugs, his father is gone... The whole thing spins out of control and accelerates down a hill without brakes...
>
> **Boyland**: You just passed the humanity test, my friend. If you didn't come out of there feeling sick, then we wouldn't be having this conversation. I couldn't talk to you. You wouldn't understand. You look a little shell-shocked.
>
> I'll tell you my story. I grew up in the worst part of Detroit, and our gang—12-year-olds— was switching from BB guns to .22s. Then my parents moved to Akron. We lived in a not-very-nice part of town. I was walking to school on my first day and a kid came up beside me, put a gun to my head, and explained he wasn't going to kill me this time because I was new in the neighborhood but if he ever caught me on that side of the street again, I'd be dead.

Kearny Mesa Juvenile Detention Facility – San Diego, CA

Born, Not Raised

Kearny Mesa Juvenile Detention Facility – San Diego, CA

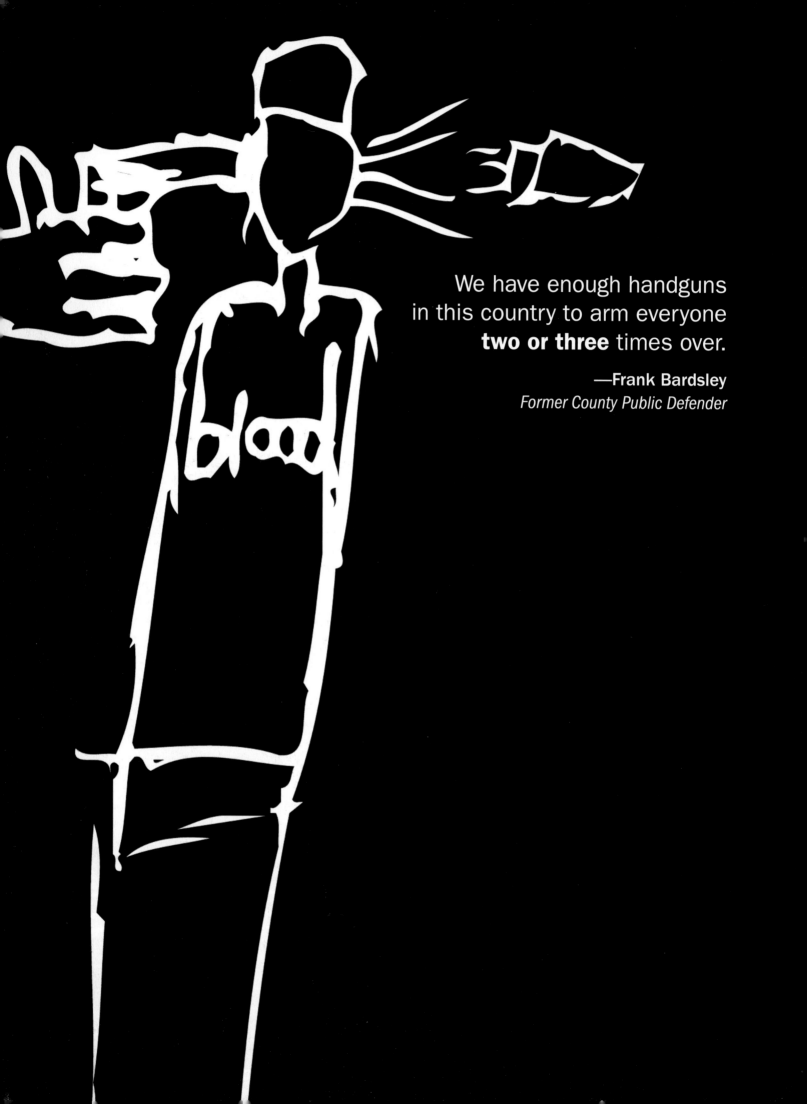

We have enough handguns in this country to arm everyone **two or three** times over.

—Frank Bardsley
Former County Public Defender

...And so I fled. I was lucky enough to find my way to a house under a freeway overpass owned by the General Tire Company and used for inner-city kids. That's what saved me. So what do you want to talk about?

Susan: Juvenile Hall is like a holding tank?

Boyland: Yes, it's a place of initial confinement. It's called detention. Kids are arrested or detained because the act they committed is too serious for dependency. Juvenile Hall is under Probation. It's the delinquency side of the court. The dependency side is social services. You won't find social services in Juvenile Hall unless it's for special cases. So when you think delinquency think Probation and when you think dependency think the Department of Social Services.

When an adult goes to jail, that adult is in the custody of the Sheriff. That's jail. Prison, on the other hand, is a place of punishment and confinement run by state agents called the Department of Corrections. They are absolutely different things.

With kids, it's almost the same as adults. They're held in a detention center—Juvenile Hall, the equivalent of jail for adults—until the legal proceedings are over. Based on the sophistication of the crime, the youth is either remanded to the Hall for a couple of months or sent to a longer-term facility by the probation department. Therefore—again like jail for adults—the Hall is both a place of pretrial confinement and a place of punishment, for shorter stays.

We also have boot-camp facilities—mostly for younger juvenile boys—located in Campo.

When a judge declares a child a ward of the court—a special legal status in our society—the court interferes with what would normally be parental rights over that child. The court becomes like the child's parent. However, the way it is today, when the judge places a child on probation but allows him to live at home or with a relative, Johnny walks out of the building and already knows that the probation officer won't come around. "Hey, it's cool, man, I'm back on the streets, let's go do whatever."

Susan: So the next time they come in, it's with a different attitude?

Boyland: Each time it's a little worse. Each time, they've learned a little more about how to avoid the system. This is offensive to me as a lawyer because I believe in the rule of law that says dependent children and delinquent children should receive services.

"Services" is a real important word in this business. Johnny, the delinquent, and Tommy, the dependent child, have been taken over by the court. Their parents have been found unable or unfit to raise them, so the court, the social-service delivery system, probation, and the Department of Social Services are supposed to give those children the services that they need. For the dependent child, it may mean finding him a new home.

I'll play judge with you for a minute. The worst service you can get as a judge is Juvenile Court. Judges play politics in the judicial community. The top dog is the administrative dog, the presiding judge, who decides which judges go to which service—criminal, probate, civil, family law, juvenile law. The real prestige is to be appointed downtown and handle the most prestigious work, civil suits. To handle money. It's hard to attract judges to Juvenile Court.

It's equally hard to attract attorneys. A deputy district attorney sees Juvenile Court as purgatory. You want to be downtown, doing the real felonies, getting your name in the paper. Thank god there are some lawyers who want to do this work, who really believe they can make a difference. Try to get a kid on a good life path instead of a bad life path.

> The child's system, the delinquency system, is supposed to stress rehabilitation of the child, not punishment.
>
> —Bill Boyland
> *Former Chief Deputy Public Defender*

The juvenile delinquent system is a deprivation of a child's liberty to become a decent adult. It's our job as defense lawyers to pull the child out of the system. Sometimes making a difference means getting the child the right kind of services so that the psychological problem can be solved and the educational problem solved, because 40 percent of these children have severe educational issues. The problem is, it's expensive to fix kids. Society plays great lip service to, "These are our children, they're the hope of tomorrow, they're the next generation," but we don't spend any money to accomplish it. As lawyers, we see them using the cheapest solutions and sending the kids to boot camps because it's an easy and inexpensive way to house a child for a set period of time. It's the cheapest thing the county can do with a child.

The game's getting tighter. I've been doing this for six years now. Two things are happening at the same time. One is that juvenile misconduct is increasing due to forces we all understand—guns and drugs. At the same time, the amount of money being spent on kids is being reduced. So that means more kids will commit more serious acts and end up in non-rehabilitative confinement.

The adult system stresses punishment—you did wrong and we've got to punish you to teach you a lesson and protect the community. We've got to put a wall around you so you won't get out and rape Mrs. Jones.

The child's system, the delinquency system, is supposed to stress rehabilitation of the child, not punishment. But we aren't giving treatment to Johnny—who committed a sex offense—for sexually acting out. We'll confine him, but we won't rehabilitate him, and he'll come out either a child molester or a rapist.

The judge is in a box because the county doesn't have enough money to pay for expensive treatment for this child. We're loading everything on the next generation. They'll have to pay the debts that we ran up, doing things the dumb way, not engaging in preventative action.

This interview took place a number of years ago. This past year, San Diego witnessed what Boyland predicted can happen when John Albert Gardner III confessed to the rape and murder of two teenage girls and the assault of other teens who were lucky enough to escape. Convicted a decade earlier, at age 20, of assaulting a 13-year-old neighbor, he served time then, but received no treatment.

Communities were outraged as the recent story unfolded and the horror of the harsh reality sank in. Parents panicked and were terrified to let their daughters walk unescorted in broad daylight. The media obsessed on these sensational crimes until the passage of Chelsea's Law, which provides for a life-without-parole sentence for the worst child molesters, but also offers ongoing treatment for paroled sex offenders deemed eligible for rehabilitation.

Will sufficient funds be available for rehabilitation? In the realm of juvenile justice, the Probation Department simply has no money to initiate the positive programs that Mack Jenkins, the current and brilliant Chief Probation Officer, knows only too well would work to educate at-risk youths and halt criminal behavior early in life through training, remediation, and literacy.

As I worked my way toward access to Juvenile Hall, I began to get a real sense of the problems confronting the attorneys as well as the judges in the overtaxed system of juvenile justice. By this time, my daughter Polly had decided to join me in the project, and we were able to schedule a meeting with the

My experience at the hotle...

My experience at the hotle when my boyfriend close friend got shot. It's a day i'll never forget. Well we used to stay in a hotle for a couple of day's and we had two hotle rooms at that hotle and my boyfriend friend would go there to kick it and one night something went down and my boyfriend got into some trouble. So one of my boyfriends friend got a shot gun and he's kind of goofy so we told him don't put no bullets in it so he took then out and then for some reason he put then back in and a friend came and we were in the onewer me and my boyfriend and all we heard was a big "BOOM" so we went out and we thought they were messing around but then we seen my boyfriend friend laying on the bed he was in shock so i told my boyfriend to take him to the hospital so we took him and he got shot right above his but whole. and i told then see what happened for being around guns. It was a big scene i don't want to ever be around guns cause you never know what could happend.

Maria Minton (girl), age 15

Packet Number: 19   **Unit:** 400
                                                        Age: 16

1) Is this your first time being in Juvenile Hall? If not, how many times have you been there? 2 onee for a half day

a) Is Juvenile Hall like you thought it would be? Why/why not?
yes crapy from the pepole

b) When you get out of Juvenile Hall what would you like to accomplish for other young people so they don't have to experience Juvenile Hall?
tri to tell them to stop thare bad ways

2) Do you think after your release, you'll come back if not, what will you do to make sure you won't return? turn good all the way

3) Are you in school? If not do you have any plans to go back and finish?
yes

4) Do you have a positive role model that you can talk to?
NO

5) Do you have any family members that have been, or are in jail or prison?
yes

6) What are your plans for the future?
?

7) What have you given deep thought to since you have been in Juvenile Hall?
Getting out and go to oklahoma

8) If you have one wish to change something in your life, what would it be?
my mom and dad's drug uses

9) Remember when you used to dream as a small child. What did you want to be when you grew up? yes

10) Have you ever been subjected to peer pressure? If so, how did it make you feel? How would you change it if you could and why?
NO

11) What was your most memorable event (in your past)?
seeing my dad sober

cat pieson by someone

Joseph Minton (boy), age 16

director of Juvenile Hall to discuss our goals.

The day of the meeting, Polly and I entered the reception area of the Hall. From behind the glass barricade, a woman asked for our driver licenses and told us to lock all other possessions in the miniature lockers housed against the back wall, just beyond the walk-through metal detector.

With a loud clank, the sallyport opened. A man dressed in relaxed uniform attire warmly greeted us from within the sallyport and invited us to join him.

"I'm Coach Tim, I'll take you to the director," he said. "Step inside."

We entered the sallyport, a passageway between reception and the Hall proper. With all sallyports I had experienced in jails—and the one at the Hall was no different—one steel door opens, allowing you entry, then closes completely, locking you inside a capsule, exposed to the control staff, until the control guard releases the grills on the opposite door.

Coach Tim explained that all guards who manage the youths in the Hall are called Coach. The young people call them by their first name and that title. Coach Tim then escorted us to the office of the director of the Hall.

A very handsome and well-dressed woman of about 50, Sara Vickers, Director of Kearny Mesa Juvenile Detention, stood at her office doorway and greeted Polly and me. She asked a couple of pertinent questions about this project, then told us to step inside her office. She moved to her desk, sat, grabbed a pen, and using it as a pointer told us to have a seat. Sara was comfortable talking to us about the Hall.

> **Susan**: Tell us about the population in Juvenile Hall.
>
> **Sara**: We have 5,000 youths on probation. When the kids come through the door of IBR— inmate booking/release—they look scared and old, haggard, and by the time you wash them up and get them out of baggy Dockers and they've seen the nurse, you see you have a child. It's surprising the difference that 20 minutes can make. Makeup is gone, hair is washed, and it's a recognizable child of 14, sometimes younger. That's what keeps people in our business chugging along. If all you see is hoods and hoodlums and proof of their crimes, you might not choose to undergo the trauma of this work, and it might be difficult to treat them as children. But they're kids!
>
> The offenses that bring them here vary. Some of the female population have acted out in order to escape an abusive, molesting home—they steal cars, anything to get away. We need to work with them individually to show them other ways of handling their problems. Some of the kids are violent; they've acted out against a victim and they're in for serious damage. We're not talking about pushing, or one small punch, a simple assault. We're talking about some real damage. Some kids are in on a warrant for running away from placement or committing a new offense.
>
> What you'll probably get a feel for very quickly is the hostility. It's depressing to see that in children. Many of them have been ignored and neglected or simply thrown away, and that's very sad. Based on the crimes they've committed, we're only trying to give them whatever rehabilitative opportunities we can, so they can reflect…
>
> **Polly**: When the doors close and they can't get out…
>
> **Sara**: It gives them a rush, like a drug addict. Violence is very addictive, and reliving the violent affair reinforces that negative behavior. Just like shooting up heroin. The rush is the reinforcement of that prior memory.
>
> We have 25 kids in here looking at 25-to-life. We have 15-year-olds being tried in adult court because of the seriousness of the crime. We have kids who come to the Hall and love being

in here. It's the first time in a long time that they've had breakfast, lunch, and dinner and been told when to brush their teeth, when to go to bed. They respond to that. What they don't respond to well is being told, "Go down to your room." We get the, "You're not the boss of me" attitude.

Sara listened to what Polly and I hoped to do with the youths during our visits. She told us that we would need to present our educational materials to her as well as to the public defender's juvenile chief, Randy Mize, for approval. We would also need to complete a three-day self-defense course at the Hall. If approved, we would receive badges as Probation volunteers. I noted the rules and instructions we had to follow:

- Seaboard training and panic button locations in classrooms
- Three-day self-defense training by staff member
- No physical confrontation, no physical intervention
- Approved release of personal information form before entering
- A letter in writing for coaches to let them know what we are doing
- No treats for the kids
- All tools must be shown to staff before we begin
- Business cards and releases to staff
- Work with each group for two-three-four weeks
- Fax names and have six alternates for public defenders with names and DOB
- Call the Deputy Chief once we have been approved by the Director

Polly and I worked as a team to create our educational materials. We carefully crafted questions for the youths that would help the public understand their educational background, family status, and history of family members incarcerated. We were interested in the number of times each young person had been in the Hall. We wanted to see how candid and creative they could be about sensitive issues such as loneliness, friends, role models, holidays. Polly created questions that pertained to her internship in psychology. I created questions geared toward family, aspirations, dreams, goals for future education and employment. Surprisingly, we constructed three different interview questionnaires in a very short timeframe. We also created photo sheets of my images and those of other professional photographers, intending to ask the youths to write about what they felt when they looked at the images. We gathered books on art and photography. Sara said we could play music during the work sessions. We were instructed to show the coaches any new supplies we planned on using—brushes, pens, crayons—as the youths were not permitted to use pens on a regular basis, for safety purposes.

Next came the three-day training. I wasn't certain what to expect. Our trainer was a kind and very strong coach. He initially introduced us to the maneuvers we were expected to master, including a full-flowered hand twist that Polly and I had to practice on each other. Initially timid about crunching her Mom's hand, Polly finally cut loose. It does hurt! And it works. We also learned a few throws onto the mat and some other safety positions. It was strenuous, but gave us a new level of appreciation for the place we hoped to encounter on our own. It's tempting to believe that kids will be decent and trusting; it's eye-opening when you're informed some of them may be dangerous.

Another several months of meetings postponed our entry. Finally, all the hurdles were behind us, and we were approved to meet with the young people in Juvenile Hall.

We have **25 kids** in here looking at **25-to-life**.

We have **15-year-olds** being tried in adult court
because of the seriousness of the crime.

We have kids who come to the Hall and
love being in here. It's the first time in a long time that
they've had breakfast, lunch, and dinner and been told
when to brush their teeth, when to go to bed.

—Sara Vickers
Former Director, Kearny Mesa Detention Facility

Kearny Mesa Juvenile Detention Facility – San Diego, CA

2

Inside the Hall
Beginnings

Take care of your kids, 'cause it sucks when no one cares.

—**Yale** (boy), resident of Juvenile Hall

The first night, following protocol, we entered the Hall with what we were allowed to bring: our bags of books, tape recorders, crayons, and paper. A coach met us at the sallyport and escorted us up and down hallways, past a control unit, and into a separate locked unit, Unit 70 for girls. These girls had cells assigned to them, but also had day-room privileges unless they were on UC—unit confinement. Girls in UC were removed from their locked-down cells only for specified appointments and visitations, not for any social or educational events.

The coach positioned us before a group of about 50 young women. They sat at tables of eight, gawking at us and wearing expressions remarkable for their disinterest and distrust. At a glance, over half the girls appeared Hispanic or of mixed Hispanic/African American ethnicity; another 25 percent were Asian, with whites in the minority.

The blank expressions and stifled laughter behind covered mouths told me that this would be a tough audience to reach. To penetrate such barriers would take major breakthroughs. I asked myself, *Why do you do this stuff?*

Then I started talking.

"I'm a photographer and writer and I want to interview young people going through an incarceration process. My daughter is in her last semester at the university and is receiving credit for participation. We have photos, books, interviews to share with you all. We also hope to have time to talk in groups about what it's like to be in the Hall.

"I brought in a newspaper; I'm aware you don't have newspapers here. There's a famous photographer—his name is Roy DeCarava, and I studied with him 10 years ago. This article was written about him in yesterday's *L.A. Times*, because a Los Angeles museum is having a retrospective of DeCarava's images. He said, 'All you have to do is be,' meaning he didn't think we should place unrealistic expectations on young people. He believed that people ought to be the people they are. His photos reflect this philosophy. His work is very freeing. I want you all to see his work. And we have other artists to share with you girls tonight, too."

Polly passed the articles and photo books around to the girls of Unit 70. One of the articles was about animals.

"Does anyone here have a pet?" Polly asked.

Many girls raised their hands.

"Let's all take a turn with this."

"I have a Rottweiler. His name is Yesterday."

"I have a pit bull named Fido."

"I have a bird. I have cats, too."

So many of these kids...
Dad not there, Mom with no parenting
skills. It's amazing. When I was working
in Probation outside the Hall, there were
kids looking for dope at four a.m.
They were brazen.
Young people are different on drugs.

—Coach Kristen

"I got a dog named Snoopy."

We had broken through the distancing veil.

Then Coach Kim stepped in to check on us. "Quiet down, you can hardly hear when she's talking to you!"

Another girl shouted out over the coach, "Two dogs, a rabbit, a bird, a fish!"

The girls were eagerly sharing. We passed around some books. Several girls looked through the book of photographs by André Kertész. The genuine romance of days gone by intrigued them. One girl opened the Georgia O'Keefe book and studied each image of her paintings.

Later, we talked to two of the coaches. Their comments told us a lot about the sources of suffering in the lives of these girls.

Coach Kristen: For the most part, these girls are all abused. They're not really bad people, but they just keep doing things to call attention to the fact they need help. That's called a status offender. They're children of people who say they want to be good parents, but they let their kids slide. Parents need to have very clear lines of what is and is not acceptable and say, "This is what's going to happen if you go left of the line," and God willing, they don't say it in anger! To say, "If you run away again you won't step foot in my house," is stupid. That's the same as saying, "I'm never going to help you again." We have kids all the time flip us off. They say, "I don't have to listen to anybody, why do I have to listen to you? Just spray me!" I don't want to have to use pepper spray on any of them. The spray gets on me too!

Coach Kristen explained that there were very smart kids who were in the Hall for very serious crimes—murder, even—yet were outstanding students. Then there were those willing to help with laundry and kitchen duties who were resigned to their fate and shrugged: I am in an institution, and this is what my life is going to be.

Coach Kristen: So many of these kids... Dad not there, Mom with no parenting skills. It's amazing. When I was doing probation outside the Hall, the kids were brazen, looking for dope at four a.m. Young people are different on drugs. They're not looking for their folks. Then after they're off drugs and cleaned up, they tell me, "Oh man, I get scared." Drugs are really a plague on society.

That night, leaving Unit 70, I wondered how many of the girls would end up with a life of limited education and eventual incarceration, or in abusive relationships.

During our next visit, we were escorted to a private interview room. An unfamiliar coach approached us with Morinski, a big girl, a little mannish looking, who plodded along the corridor, dulled by the mission of meeting someone for a random visit. She entered the oversized booth and sat down at the small table. Initially, she didn't want to talk or work. She stared at Polly with a challenging, flat expression. Polly broke the silence.

Polly: Are you associated with a gang?
Morinski: Yeah. Friends come and go. The family doesn't. The gang's like a family. It never comes and goes. It's like they're there for the rest of your life. I created my own pack. I was a Crip. The difference with me, I was friends with a head Blood, Essays. Throughout all the groups it was weird. I was friends even regardless of where I was. It didn't matter.

Kearny Mesa Juvenile Detention Facility – San Diego, CA

We discovered Morinski was fearful that she might be pregnant.

> **Morinski**: I'm late, two months. I been pregnant before. I feel the same—nausea. I had a miscarriage, twins. Happened last year when I was 15. I was raped when I was 11. It took four years to have sex after that. I got pregnant.
> **Polly**: Why don't girls wait to have sex?
> **Morinski**: I honestly think they wanna fit in and talk about something. Be part of the crowd. It's a shame.

Although the visit was short, when the coach returned for her, Morinski said she would think about writing and maybe have something for us on our the next visit. It surprised Polly and me that Morinski shifted from being unwilling to talk into discussing such a personal subject as pregnancy and sex. It was clear she hadn't been able to warm up to adults in quite some time.

A few moments later, Coach Janet brought in a stunning, tall 16-year-old, Steinley, who once again broke the stereotype of what we imagined a young woman in Juvenile Hall would be like. Articulate, focused, and engaging, Steinley immediately was interested in writing.

When I asked what she liked to write about she quickly responded, "Sometimes I write stories with a lot of qualities in the character. Sometimes the characters will even have some of my characteristics."

As she wrote, she talked about her stay in the Hall.

> **Steinley**: I hate the judge. He doesn't understand. I lived in New York for 11 years and then I moved to California with my mom at 15. Now, it's going to be a while, probably get two years. I guess I've made myself adjust to everything in here. Usually I'd be whining, not used to a place like this, but I took to it pretty quick 'cause I felt that I had to. There are a lot of girls in here are gonna come in and go and I'm gonna still be here when they aren't.

When she shared with us her special love for her mother, we gave her an assignment—"What it means to be a daughter." Her move from New York must have been traumatic. She did not appear to like San Diego.

The final interview of the evening was with Barnes. Definitely a confident tomboy, Barnes gave the impression in the private interview room of someone happy to see us and willing to talk, share, and express her ideas. Of medium height, she had long strawberry blond hair, loads of freckles, and bright blue eyes.

> **Susan**: You like to write about yourself?
> **Barnes**: Yeah. And my family. I wrote about a beast going into my sister's room and she could hear him breathing and coming up the stairs, calling out to her. He opened the door and ripped her with claws. He's got big beastly hands and he's ugly and he just takes over her fragile little body and mentally and physically damages her. It's really about my dad molesting my sister and then he locks the door with a latch and she sits there and cries and no one helps her. It just makes me really mad.
>
> I've had like two and a half years of messing around, doing drugs. I have at least a year of recovery.
>
> I'm stressing. I saw my family today in court. My stepdad kicked butt for me and sat with my two lawyers. My stepdad and my sisters were there and this is a really hardcore judge—Lassiter. It's embarrassing to go in court shackled, hands tagged up around your waist and feet shackled. You have to stay like that and they're all lookin' at you. It's embarrassing. They think like I'm gonna murder somebody.
> **Susan**: Was it hard for your stepdad to see you like that?
> **Barnes**: No. He was makin' fun of it. "Can I buy a pair of those and bring them home?"

As a child her father told her that she had a special gift. And a year later he died. Being so young she never questioned him on what exactly he meant, so she didn't know what her gift was. As she grew up, she made it her personal goal to understand her father, his words and their meanings.

She wrote day in and day out, about her feelings, the loss of her father, and her life. She felt confused and worthless, because as everyone worked on their own interests and hobbies, she in return didn't know what hers were. She stopped paying attention in school and instead wrote in her journal. One particular day, the teacher caught her. The girl broke out in tears, telling her teacher that she couldn't do anything right and she wasn't anything special, because she didn't know her gift like everyone else. The teacher read her writings and looked up astonished. Then she broke out into a laughter. "Your gift is right in front of you and you've been looking over it this whole time."

The girl recieved a scholarship to a prodigous college, because of her excellent talent in writing. She wrote several books and went on to become a famous author. Years later, going through her father's old notes, she found a letter from her father to her. It wrote "My daughter, the excellent author, you have found your gift." She smiled her poodle Sammy close by, and sat down with pride.

Gertrude Stein © Estate of Horst P. Horst / Art + Commerce   Steinley (girl), age 16

Hi, my name is Chris. Im 36 years old. I live in Salem Oregon on a beautiful ranch. I have a gorgious wife and two lovely children. One girl (3) named Tabitha and a studly boy (8) named Micheal, Im a average white guy with a childish personality. I enjoy spending most of my time playing with my children whenever Im not working. Im town doctor and earn a good salary. Im a friendly person and everyone in town knows me. Its a small town and a very small world. My greatest sucsess is becoming a doctor. My biggest failure is when I lost my first patient 5 years ago. He went into cardiac arrest. There was nothing I could do. It was his time to go but I can't live down the guilt. During my quiet time after the kids have gone to sleep I sit in my lazy chair and enjoy a glass of wine while reading my favorite novels by Dean Koontz, then I go upstairs, get into bed and fall into a nice sleep with my wife in my arms. On March 3 I got up, it was a beautiful day, I did my typical day routine. But today I was taking the day off. I had told my wife and children that I would stay home and help paint the house. We started with Tabithas room. We dressed in our worse clothes and went to work. While we were painting I hadnt noticed that Micheal had wandered off. About ½ an hour later I smelt smoke, fire smoke. What I had forgotten is that Micheal had turned into a typical pyro. He had started a fire in the barn. I droped everything and ran outside grabed the hose and put it out, it was the most frightening moment in my life. Thank-God it wasnt too late,

Barnes (girl), age 15

People saying, "Can I give you a hand?" No, it wasn't fun for me. Talking to my lawyer with everybody walking by looking at me like I was a criminal. I said, "See? There's a sign around my neck, I'm not guilty." I stole a street sign. My lawyer says that most drug rehabs are a year-long program. I'm no longer a delinquent 'cause I have a whole different family case that's been there for two years.

Barnes leaned back in the bucket chair and started to talk freely about her experiences, her personality and character. Listening to this young girl, Polly and I were completely captivated. Her thought processes and her interpretation of life incidents seemed way beyond her years; it was difficult to fathom how she could be so articulate when she was also such a victim.

Barnes: I've grown up with guys. I don't really like hanging out with girls. I played on the Little League team, played soccer in junior high. I live here with girls now. I have to cope. I can't "not like it."

I did crystal meth for three years. My mom and dad got a divorce after 17 years and my mom went downhill. She hadn't held a job and had five kids and thought she could take care of them. And then my dad got charged with molesting my sister and none of the kids could live with my dad. My mom started going to bars, drinking and tweaking. She'd never had social workers in her life before and if your dad has sexual molestation charges filed, social workers are in your life.

We used to have a two-story house and went hiking up the mountain on the trails. I was a little tomboy with BB guns. We'd sneak around. We were spies. We loved it. We'd go and steal snacks. It was a nice house. I'm my father and mother's only real child. Oh, I have a younger sister, two younger brothers and three older sisters. My mom has a child, my step-sister or half-sister. *Plus* we adopted four kids from the same family; they're all real brothers and sisters. Foster kids for six years. So it was like one big happy family for five years.

Polly: School?

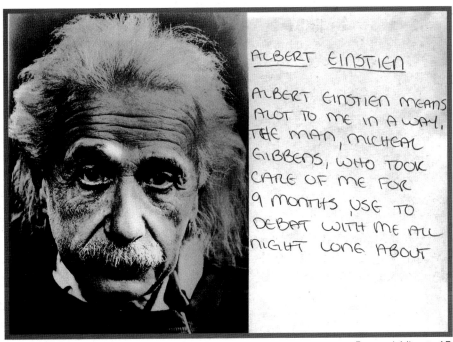

Photo by Philippe Halsman © Halsman Archive

Barnes (girl), age 15

Barnes: I started one day of school in 9th. From then on I slept on the streets, in bushes, in vacant houses. I was kinda homeless.

I handed her some photo cards Polly and I had picked out from a kiosk at a local bookstore. The oversized postcards were famous photographs taken during the last 60 years.

Barnes: This reminds me of when I took my psych eval—looking at these pictures. Can I take this picture and write a story about that person? Einstein, man. Me and my buddy used to debate about Albert Einstein all night long. This is kinda weird being in this space talking to you guys. My buddy saw me on the streets and took care of me. He told me to lean on him, that it's people that are important. He still works at Lockheed Martin. He lives with his dad or even in a truck still. He doesn't like to settle down. We like to road trip a lot and we went to Oregon.

Susan: He's 36 and doesn't have a home?
Barnes: He doesn't like houses. He's had like three wives and he has a son.
Susan: But he didn't lay a hand on you?
Barnes: Never once said a sexual word with me.
Susan: In 52 days you've read how many books?
Barnes: I've read *Stranger in a Mirror*, *Shadows* by John Saul, *Old Yeller* 'cause I never seen that movie. It was depressing. I cried. I've read more. Several books by Dean Koontz. I picture them in my head. I see each one like a movie.

Polly: What's changing for you?
Barnes: It's nice to hear nice things about yourself when you just hate yourself. I'm just now starting to like myself. That's what we wrote about last night. I'm quick to count other people's faults, but seldom think about how I hurt other people. I said I'd done drugs for a long time and my father would pick me up and I'd take right back off and I hurt my family by doing that and the people I love. I live each minute with regret and guilt. I wanna go to school and become good in something but if I mess up it's my fault.

I'm going to write about pressure. I'm sly—smart. How can they put me in jail—take me away from loved ones and not allow me to write about what I'm doing?

Barnes and Steinley selected sophisticated topics like Einstein and Proust, and wanted to express reactions to photographic images. These girls were focused and capable of great educational advancement.

Our night with them gave us a very different taste of the Hall. Their crimes did not seem to match their great gifts.

Ten days passed before our next visit in the Hall. When we returned we were escorted to the Girls' 200 Unit. A coach delivered some papers and told us they were from Morinski who had left the Hall for CYA (California Youth Authority) placement. When we returned we were escorted to the Girls' 200 Unit. We settled into the unit. Several girls passed our table, making faces at Connolly, the oldest girl in the unit. As a more experienced youth with a few trips to the Hall under her belt, she had a certain power. There was a good deal of activity and bustling around in the unit. Two other girls came closer to us, cautiously interested in who we were and what we were doing in the Hall.

A very tall, lean girl named Pendleton sat down next to Polly. She knew Steinley had talked to us and she seemed eager to share. "I miss Steinley. She was moved," Pendleton reported. "They got her at five o'clock in the morning. She was all excited. She said, 'I get to do my time.'"

Webster, a short, overweight teen with a bad case of acne joined us.

(ADULT)

A puppy or dog. Sitting maybe waiting for it's owner. Maybe that person abandoned it's special animal. A lost soul could be like a puppy. Wandering, searching, waiting to be touched, loved, or carassed. Wanting a home. Waiting for security and a lil food.
Loyal and abeident, trained, and in training. Like a child.

This young....... well actually old woman looks as though her life has been so rough. I think you took this picture to share the pain of her face. So stern and not trusting. Scared to believe anymore. Maybe she feels like there is no hope anymore. She looks like she waits for something special or bad to happen. Struggling with emotions she wants to hide or has hidden for a long time. I think she wonders am I real. Am I a person who desires things. Am I special. "HER THOUGHTS" "Will or can I obtain these things."

Morinski (girl), age 16

Susan: How long have you been in here, Webster?

Webster: Seven months. Six more months to go.

Another Coach entered and warned, "Ladies—quiet down." Connolly let us know she was the most mature and would talk to us, but would not write or fill in questionnaires.

Susan: Yet you wanted to do this project.

Connolly: 'Cause I haven't been lying. I'm finishing high school and that's it. I might not go to college, period. It depends on what my life's got ahead. I never even thought about going to college. I never thought about graduating high school, June 9. I never thought the day would come. I'm not really thrilled about it. Maybe when the day happens but right now it's just a graduation. I'm just done with high school; that's about it. I never thought I'd live to this age.

Susan: You thought you'd die...on the street?

Connolly: Uh-huh. My body collapses. You know...they find a certain chemical, too much of it...my kidneys and heart just stop because of my chemical use.

Polly: Why would you use chemicals if you know that?

Connolly: Because of my habit. I'm an addict. Only time I'm sober is when I'm in here. You have no choice.

Susan: Is it hard for you to get clean?

Connolly: Yeah. Really hard.

Polly: Heroin?

Connolly: I've used every single drug out there. Choice is cocaine.

Polly: What would it take for you to want to be clean?

Connolly: I don't think about myself being clean and I know that it isn't going to happen now and it won't happen until I want it to and right now I just don't want it to.

Polly: If you were 25 years old and someone asked you, "If you were 18 and could make a decision to not use, what do you think you'd do?" What would you say?

Connolly: I don't know. When it's not in my face then I'm fine. When it's in my face then it's hard for me to say no. I've never said no to drugs.

Polly: If you knew it was your last hit and you were going to die would you still take it?

Connolly: Depends on the situation that I'm in. If I'm already drunk, I know I'd take the hit.

Polly: Are you already high when you take a hit, acting stupid?

Connolly: Yeah. Sexually aggressive. Depends on the people I'm around.

Susan: Do you like that image of yourself?

Connolly: Doesn't bother me. That's my lifestyle.

With each answer she raised her right eyebrow and looked at us, testing us.

Later, as we headed down the corridor to Unit 200, a coach, escorting Pendleton, stopped us and handed us Pendleton's work. Pendleton remained quiet and distant, knowing we had her work in hand.

Back in Unit 200, Coach Yvette said there were 57 girls in the unit, many of whom had been in the juvenile system multiple times. "So, it isn't working. And a lot of these girls are in here for prostitution."

Coach Donna, a short camp-like counselor, stepped up to share her thoughts about the at-risk kids in the Hall.

Coach Donna: We have kids who say they are schizo and on psych meds. They'll play it, thinking it looks good in the courts. Juveniles tried for murder as adults, life and no parole, they may end up on suicide watch. It's a rude awakening because they can't go to the bathroom without permission. First time here, it's hard. And having to do it in front of everybody. Locked in a room all day, nothing to do. They become "institutionalized," meaning dependent on an institution for their existence. It's what happens to them.

Susan: That doesn't sound like a lot of hope. It must be hard to watch.

Coach Donna: For example, in the Girls' Segregated Unit—that's a unit where girls are locked in cells all day and monitored—we had twins. Their brother was also on our case list. One of the girls was dating a guy from one gang. The sister was dating a guy from another gang but they were from mixed-family parents and mixed nationalities. The mother was a prostitute and the father an alcoholic. There was a stepfather, too. They got released and didn't have a chance with the parents. They were institutionalized, again. All three are in here on a gang case. Parents are never home.

We have a 15-year-old, dyslexic, can't read. His crime is high profile, in the news, for doing a vicious act. He's really quiet. He'll say, "Coach, can you read this to me?" The world doesn't know what they're going through, but as an officer you get a better feel of what the kids go through. These are all kids in the San Diego community! In Unit 1200, the boys look like babies, like eight-year-olds, they're so small. They're needy.

Coach Donna showed compassion for these youths, knowing they hadn't had a decent upbringing, loving family, fair education, or solid relationships. In many cases, they were so far removed from normal family bonds that they needed to be institutionalized. The Hall became their home, the only environment with safe boundaries.

It's a rude awakening because they can't go
to the bathroom without permission.
First time here, it's hard.
And having to do it in front of everybody.
Locked in a room all day, nothing to do.
They become "institutionalized,"
meaning dependent on an institution for their existence.
It's what happens to them.

—Coach Donna

Kearny Mesa Juvenile Detention Facility – San Diego, CA

"The Humming bird"

The humming bird flew from wall to wall, not knowing where to go. All scared in an unfamiliar surrounding. Trying to find light but seeing only darkness. He was flying for 2 hours. When he got tired, he fell. The coach picked him up and put him outside. A few minutes later, she went to go check on him, but he was gone. Although he left behing a souvenier. It was one of his tiny feathers. IF I was the humming bird I would of been really scared. - But maybe the actual humming bird wasn't scared. He probably came for a reason, maybe in the form of an actual humming bird. Maybe he was a messenger for one of us, maybe from God, maybe from the devil. Maybe its someones gaurdian angel watching over them, but only in a life form. I don't know. Im ending it here.

Chim (girl), age 15

3

Girls' Rehabilitation Facility
Table Talk

If I was the old man [in the Tolstoy story] I would have told them this isn't right. I don't want to be treated like a dog. I may not have teeth but I'm a human being.

— **Chim** (girl), resident of GRF, Juvenile Hall

The Girls' Rehab Facility—GRF—is a unit designed for girls needing treatment for drug abuse and/or preparing for reentry into society. The girls we visited in this unit moved in and out of GRF from Unit 70 based on their behavior. This unit had a small conference room where we could set up music, supplies, and have an open session with three or more girls at a time. Often, the girls ate their dinner during our visits.

We had met with four girls—Hui, Chim, Minton, and Sands—once a week for six weeks. One day Hui, Chim, and Minton told us that Sands wasn't able to join us. Sands had done something to earn her AR status—Administrative Removal. The other girls were pretty down. They sat around the small conference table acting bored, yet we sensed they felt otherwise. Mood swings were commonplace with these kids.

> **Susan**: Hui, you told us that you aren't from San Diego originally. Where are you from?
> **Hui**: My mom is Laotian. My dad's Cambodian so I'm mixed.
>
> **Polly**: You seem pretty down.
> **Hui**: That's because I hate this place and I think I'm here for 210 days [pauses]. It wasn't drug related. It was a mistake. Things just happened and so I'm paying for it.
> **Polly**: Your first time here?
> **Hui**: Yeah, but both of my brothers...well, one is gone in CYA [now DJJ, Department of Juvenile Justice] and the other one is in 1400 Unit, all on the same case, so it's hard. Plus, me and Chim are in here on the same case.
> **Polly**: What year are you in school?
> **Hui**: I went to school for like three or four months until I got locked up. I'm 14 and in high school. I like school.
>
> **Susan**: Do you like to write?
> **Hui**: Yeah. I like to write about other people. I like to write essays.
>
> **Polly**: What else do you like?
> **Hui**: I like curry and chicken with rice. I like it really hot. I like cooking.

Once we acknowledged that we all missed Sands, Hui and Chim loosened up. Sands had provided them with a feisty glow. They often sparred with Sands; mostly that was an act and yet, without Sands present, it was harder for Hui and Chim to be open with us. Minton was indifferent about Sands not being there. Still, the relative lack of structure during our meetings was refreshing to the girls.

> The grandfather had become very old. His legs wouldn't go, his eyes didn't see, his ears didn't hear, he had no teeth. And when he ate, the food dripped from his mouth.
>
> The son and daughter-in-law stopped setting a place for him at the table and gave him supper in back of the stove. Once they brought dinner down to him in a cup. The old man wanted to move the cup and dropped and broke it. The daughter-in-law began to grumble at the old man for spoiling everything in the house and breaking the cups and said that she would now give him dinner in a dishpan. The old man only sighed and said nothing.
>
> Once the husband and wife were staying at home and watching their small son playing on the floor with some wooden planks: he was building something. The father asked: "What is that you are doing, Misha?" And Misha said: "Dear Father, I am making a dishpan. So that when you and dear Mother become old, you may be fed from this dishpan."
>
> The husband and wife looked at one another and began to weep. They became ashamed of so offending the old man, and from then on seated him at the table and waited on him.

my point of view

This segmant of a longer story almost shows Karma (what goes around comes around). But once the couple saw that it wasnt right to do what they did they stopped.

The old mans point of view: "Damn! I cant believe these people. I could of sworn I was human, not an animal! Well, I should be thankful that im still alive. This really isnt right, should I tell them how i feel, no, maybe it's too much for them to have to worry about an old man like me."

Chim (girl), age 15

Chim: I bet Sands'll throw a fit in AR.
Susan: Why is that?
Chim: She's just that way, real touchy. Like she owns the joint.

We gave Chim a story, "The Old Grandfather and His Little Grandson," a traditional European tale as retold by by the great Russian writer Leo Tolstoy. She grabbed the printout and read it fast.

What goes around comes around. If somebody comes up at me foul I'm going to come back at them foul. My very first fight was at four.

—**Chim** (girl), age 15

Chim: If I was the couple I wouldn't do that. If I was the old man I would have felt the same way. Instead of keeping it in I would have told them this isn't right. I don't want to be treated like a dog. I may not have teeth but I'm a human being.
Susan: The old man was once young and had vital thoughts. I wonder how he treated his own dad.
Chim: What goes around comes around even if it's not right away, but years later.
Susan: "What goes around comes around." That's mentioned a lot. Do you really believe that? Or is this a gang-related concept?
Chim: Nobody's perfect. Things that happen to me, yeah, I do them to other people. What goes around comes around. If somebody comes up at me foul I'm going to come back at

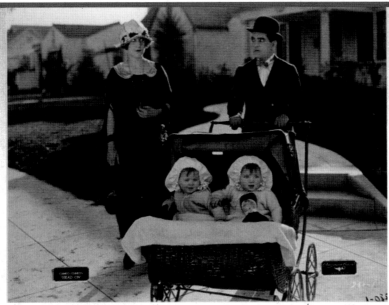

This is a Kodak moment. This is a picture of Mary and John going on a walk with ~~they~~ their twin children Lily and Ann. Lily and Ann are amazed and attracted to the beautiful sights of the world, but not everything though. Ann, on the left, wet her diapers and dont feel good. ~~Ann~~ Lily, on th right, is staring at a big dog. John and Mary are arguing about what ~~get to~~ will be done at Mary's Mother's house. John personally dont like Mary's Mom (his mother-in law.) But She wants to see her grandkids. Mary disapproves of Johns attitude. John ended up having a bad day. He didnt get any dinner and ended up sleeping up on the couch for 2 nights.

Chim (girl), age 15

them foul. My very first fight was at four. It wasn't at school but at home in front of the house, on the street with somebody my age. I remember everything. We're friends now, but I used to really hit her.

Polly: What did she do to irritate you?

Chim: She lived right across the street from me and this one day we were both wearing red skirts. Mine was faded *[laughs]*. So she called me a bum. And then she made fun of my dad 'cause her dad and my dad were real close. They expected us to be close, too. But when we walked up the street together she said, "Look at your dad's pants. He's all ugly, too. His pants are gray. And my dad's pants are black. That's why your whole family's a bum." I looked at her and said, "You don't have to say that to me or I'll hit you." She spit on my face. I smacked her.

My dad thought we were just playing. Until blood came out…

I didn't know much English then but I could cuss. I learned English from the TV. See, I was born in Thailand and came here when I was two. My dad speaks English better than my mom.

The girls wrote on selected topics, quietly, and then Chim started to talk about some serious anger issues troubling her. She said she truly "felt hate" for someone.

Susan: Could you ever see yourself really hurting somebody?
Chim: Like, kill somebody? Yes. Yeah.
Susan: I couldn't see you doing that.
Chim: That's good. Why aren't more cops like that? There was this one day when I was just walking down the street. I had a pink bag on my arm and a couple of cops asked, "Where you from? You just rob a house?" I go, "No… I don't do that. I just go to the park to get some fresh air." Another time I didn't do anything. I just sat outside the house with a baseball bat. They thought I was going to beat somebody up. They think it's all gang affiliated.

Polly: What are the advantages of being in a gang?
Chim: It's love. It's love from the people that are in. You need a place to stay, you need food, they give you food. You need money, they give you money. They give you as much love as you need. I know they're not blood related but I consider them family.

I couldn't help but hear the hurt in this child's voice as she tried to convince us that a gang could offer the same type of love that a family could for their child.

Hui took the printed-out story on 11"-by-17" paper with plenty of room for the girls to write on. She remained quiet. Minton returned from getting her dinner plate. She seemed happy, a new presence. On earlier visits, Minton hadn't wanted to contribute to the conversation. This night was different because, as she told us, "Tonight I get to see my dad!" She hadn't seen her father in seven years.

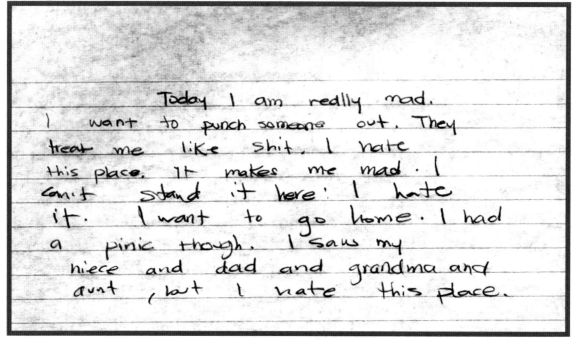

Today I am reallly mad. I want to punch someone out. They treat me like shit. I hate this place. It makes me mad. I can.t stand it here. I hate it. I want to go home. I had a pinic though. I saw my niece and dad and grandma and aunt, but I hate this place.

Hui (girl), age 15

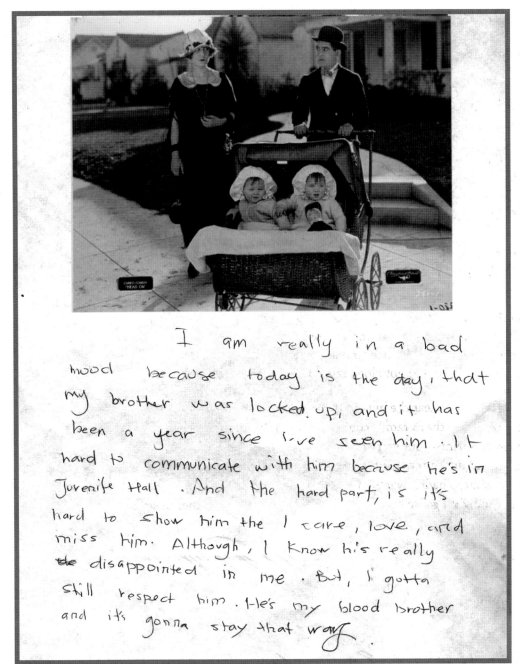

I am really in a bad mood because today is the day, that my brother was locked up, and it has been a year since I've seen him. It hard to communicate with him because he's in Juvenile Hall. And the hard part, is its hard to show him the I care, love, and miss him. Although, I know his really disappointed in me. But, I gotta still respect him. He's my blood brother and it's gonna stay that way.

Hui (girl), age 15

Polly: You were just a little girl then. You think you'll recognize him?
Minton: When I see him, I'll know it's my dad.

Hui started interrupting and grew more and more upset.

Hui: It's been six months and almost eight hours and I'm getting tired of this place.
Susan: Do you think this has to do with the fact that some of the people you're close to have gone home already?
Hui: No! I don't get close to no one here. I don't got no reason to get close to anyone I don't consider a friend. It makes me real mad when people say, "You're my friend," when I'm not really their friend. I don't like anybody in this place.

It seems like **nothing** will really help
me out because they sit down
and talk to me for hours
and it goes in one ear
and out the other.

—**Hui** (girl), age 15

This wasn't the impression she gave last week, when she and Sands were joking around together. These girls were so sensitive with one another, and easily hurt over the slightest criticism.

We moved on to another subject.

> **Polly**: Last time we saw you, you talked about boys hitting. Is it common for boys to slap girls?
>
> **Chim**: Oh yeah. When I came in I had a black eye and a bump here.

> **Susan**: You call this a boyfriend?
>
> **Hui**: Ex-boyfriend. This was all over alcohol. It was 9:15 at night, December 23 when I was incarcerated. I don't belong in a place like this. But it don't matter. It's been six months and eight hours and some minutes since the last time I seen my play brother doing 80 to life.
>
> **Chim**: He's a tight homie that you consider a brother.
>
> **Hui**: But this person's real tight because my mom consider him like a son. She loves him.
>
> **Chim**: He's doing life.

> **Susan**: So you didn't have two real brothers here.
>
> **Hui**: I did have two real brothers here.

> **Susan**: Now it's three boys here?
>
> **Hui**: Actually more.
>
> **Chim**: Sniper...and...
>
> **Hui**: Uh-huh...don't even bring up Sniper. I'm just tired of this damn place. I hope one day it explodes.

> **Polly**: What do you think will help you handle this time in the Hall?
>
> **Hui**: It seems like nothing will really help me out because they sit down and talk to me for hours and it goes in one ear and out the other.

As we left the conference room, Coach Maria, a lovely, motherly-type Hispanic woman in her mid-50s, stopped us to thank us for working with the girls. She noticed we had been talking to two gang members involved in a serious crime and possessing hot tempers.

> **Coach Maria**: We have enough problems between gang members, racial groups. That's why we have pepper spray. We have assaults. Whatever happens on the streets is brought into the Hall. If there's a gang rivalry because there's a shooting, say between two Asian gangs—we have to control those situations. We put together children of the same sophistication, maturity, age, and mentality levels—our units are broken down according to criteria that have nothing to do with what happens on the streets.

We considered that problem while we waited for someone to unlock the sallyport door for us to exit. Then we stepped out of the Hall into another beautiful night. In the dark outside, I noticed I had left the back window unzipped in the old Land Rover when we packed up to leave. I checked that open area before we got inside. This old vehicle would be great for a stowaway.

Driving off, we reviewed the evening's interviews, the friends and family members the girls had told us about—four counts of rape and murder with one young man going down for 80 years to life. Hui was in denial, not realistic about her crime, acting upset that Sands was going home and Cameron had it easy. She had had a good attitude when everybody else was down and out. But now there was no one for her, except Chim.

The Land Rover was loud as we headed away from the Hall, passing the Juvenile Courts and on past Children's Hospital. Each time we saw that hospital my mind wandered off into a memory of our youngest daughter, Samantha, as she was being wheeled into trauma surgery after having been trampled by a horse. I could smell the surgical area, the strong alcohol of the ICU as well as the inside of the small RV we had parked outside the hospital where I spent two weeks. We were so fortunate to have had our little girl pull through that horrific accident. This accident took place two weeks after the tragic car crash in front of our house when one boy was killed.

Though years had passed since those events, I found myself deeply concerned about how quickly our children can fall through our hands. In an instant, we can lose them forever. Yet my family was given a gift denied to most children in the Hall. Each time I drove by the hospital, I was reminded how little control we really have. Knowing that made the predicaments of the girls in the Hall seem that much more insurmountable.

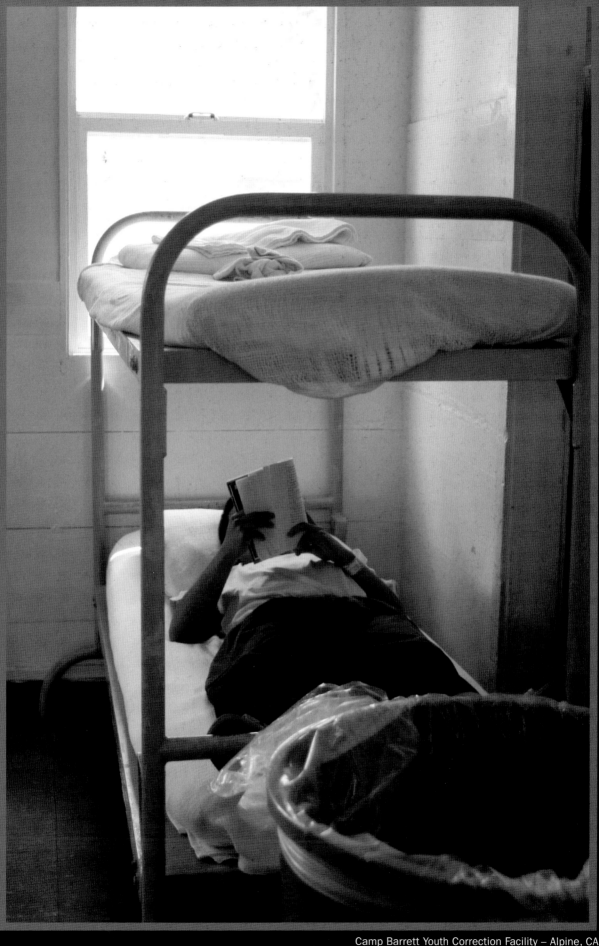

Camp Barrett Youth Correction Facility – Alpine, CA

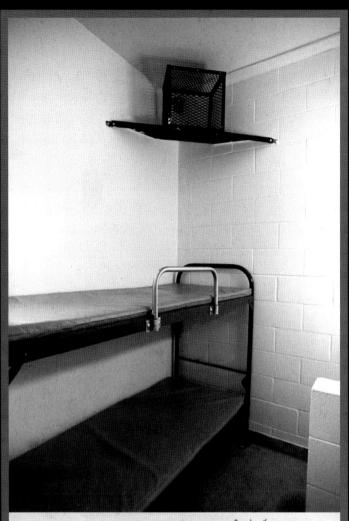

it is a rome of JAIL
that my uckle is in for
caring a hife on
him and thruxhing
my mom. Becuase he
hrt my little Brother at
home.

Beck (boy), age 14

4

The Roots of Alienation
Unmet Needs

…millions of children have some degree of impaired bonding and attachment
during early childhood. The problems that result from this can range from mild
interpersonal discomfort to profound social and emotional problems.
In general the severity of the problems is related to how early in life,
how prolonged and how severe the emotional neglect has been.

—**Bruce Perry**, M.D., Ph.D., "Bonding and Attachment in Maltreated Children"

One thing was already apparent. Many of these kids wanted to be helped. They acted as though their lives were a waste. They were of no value. But Polly and I noticed significant differences among the incarcerated youths. Those with serious attitudes that supported criminal behavior stood out in the different units as the most suspicious and unwilling to join in group activity. Icy glares and snarling chuckles beneath furled brows passed between two large Hispanic girls, for instance; these girls clearly weren't interested in whatever we had to offer. Yet those who gathered in tiny groups, snickering and pointing, were a dead giveaway; they were intrigued by a couple of ladies in street clothes they could try to relate to, somehow.

In many cases, the kids, like the incarcerated women I had interviewed, would create pseudo families among their peers. We noticed that some of the "more sophisticated criminals" were even housed among the meeker juveniles. In such a situation, how could positive change take place while the girls were incarcerated? Although Units 70, 200, and GRF were designed to deal with this issue, boundaries were obviously blurred or crossed for reasons unclear to us. Why would Sands go back and forth from Unit 70 to GRF? Why would Hui and Chim be allowed to communicate so readily if they were suspected of committing such very serious crimes?

To look for answers, I revisited Judge Milliken for a realistic chat about the future of these kids as well as to ask him why they were unable to make positive changes in their lives while incarcerated.

> **Susan**: Many of these kids are returned to a toxic environment. You're releasing them to a worse place than the Hall, yet the Hall doesn't seem to answer their needs.

> **Milliken**: That's the problem. The court needs to be the leader. Probation gives us what we want, and if we want a rigid system to warehouse kids they'll do that! Plus, there's too much emphasis on confidentiality. Parents come and sue if the files aren't sealed. Some good things are happening, but not enough. My priority is getting them out of the Hall. Scare them and then get them out.

I told Milliken what Probation Officer Henry Shankman had discussed regarding the importance of probation. Shankman had said that the increase in teen violence reflected the increase in the number of teens alienated from their families. Then, once in the system, the alienation continues. Youths in the crim-

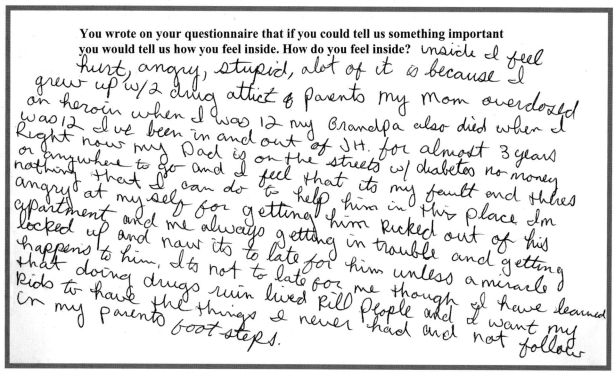

You wrote on your questionnaire that if you could tell us something important you would tell us how you feel inside. How do you feel inside? Inside I feel hurt, angry, stupid, alot of it is because I grew up w/2 drug attict of parents my mom overdozed on heroin when I was 12 my Grandpa also died when I was 12 I've been in and out of JH. for almost 3 years Right now my Dad is on the streets w/ diabetes no money or anywhere to go and I feel that its my fault and theres nothing that I can do to help him in this place I'm angry at myself for getting him kicked out of his apartment and me always getting in trouble and getting locked up and now its to late for him unless a miracle happens to him, its not to late for me though I have learned that doing drugs ruin lives kill people and I want my Kids to have the things I never had and not follow in my parents foot-steps.

Pitt (boy), age 15

inal justice system often feel an entitlement to act out as a means of dealing with their pain. This fosters even more alienation.

Milliken and I continued to identify issues wrapped around this alienation within family structure. He attributed the increased number of narcissistic personalities in the adult population of today's America to parents who fail to nurture children with love and to provide essential tools for their success. Such developmental experiences breed alienation, too.

I did some outside reading in psychology after witnessing the kids talk about the right to "get back" and "what goes around comes around." In researching the effects of alienation on the young child, I pulled up papers written by Alfred Adler and Karen Horney, along with Freud and Jung, all of whom believed that hostile, hateful personalities develop during childhood, though none claimed such hostility arose directly from a biological instinct or drive.

Seriously sociopathic individuals (adults, not youths) are categorized as having an Antisocial Personality Disorder, in which the individual is excessively impulsive, violates the rules of society, and lacks anxiety or guilt for his or her behavior. In the Hall, many youths fit the description, yet they still have not developed portions of the brain that allow for solid problem-solving and decision-making, so-called "executive functioning." Their still-developing state makes it even more important to create and sustain empathic communication with kids on the verge of falling into adult patterns of serious criminal behavior that will lead them to lifelong incarceration.

Forensic psychologist Daniel Swerdlow-Freed, Ph.D, approvingly cites the recent work of Doctors Joan Kelly and Janet Johnston, who define an alienated child as "...one who expresses, freely and persistently, unreasonable negative feelings and beliefs (such as anger, hatred, rejection, and/or fear) toward a parent that are significantly disproportionate to the child's actual experience with that parent."

In outlining some of the self-protective measures to which the abused or alienated child might turn, the neo-Freudian psychoanalyst Karen Horney (1885-1952) described mechanisms still apparent in the behavior of children in Juvenile Hall. One of these mechanisms is to achieve power and superiority over others, which counteracts the feeling that one is impotent or being mistreated. A person with an aggressive personality sees most others as being hostile and believes that only the most competent and cunning survive, so he behaves accordingly—is hateful and hostile, denigrating and abusing others—and in this manner maintains his feelings of control and power.

In their textbook *Personality: Classic Theories and Modern Research*, Howard S. Friedman and Miriam W. Schustack contrast the child raised in a loving and nurturing environment with a child raised in a violent and chaotic family in which parents beat him—not because of what he does but because they are unhappy. The growth of such an unhappy and uncared-for child is stunted and follows a predictable pattern:

> [The] boy...is ridiculed in school and ignored by his overworked teachers; is out of the mainstream and so seeks a small group of oddball friends; lives in a closed society that represses free discussion; sees people who are accused of crimes swiftly arrested, beaten, and executed; learns to view others, especially women, as mere property and servants; is taught to blindly believe all religious teachings as the road to salvation; lives in a culture where autocratic, powerful men rule by intimidation; and can find a sense of identity by adopting the ideology of a dictator and joining with other powerful forces. (Friedman and Schustack, 457)

The authors cite the work of Adler and Horney, neo-Freudian psychologists who focused on the child's early social experiences to explain aberrant patterns of alienation and violent behavior. If rejected by their parents, children may come to view the world as inhospitable and hostile; such children are more likely to grow up to be criminals. While most youngsters do experience feelings of inferiority and even rejection from time to time, the majority are able to compensate for these inferior feelings by succeeding in other areas—sports, music, friendships. But those who develop an "inferiority complex (including feelings of helplessness and incompetence) may sometimes overcompensate (developing a superiority complex), which leads them to attack and denigrate others in an attempt to increase their own feelings of importance." (Friedman and Schustack, 458)

Other research has proven that mothers who withdraw from their child's emotional needs will most likely have anxious children unable to fully develop to their potential. Lack of creative drive often derives from fear of making a mistake or not feeling good enough to earn attention from Mommy; such fear and insecurity becomes problematic for the child in school as well as in developing relationships.

When a youth enters into the criminal justice system, he or she may never have had a proper psychological assessment or opportunity for psychotherapy or even emotional support. Even when the youths have had an assessment, judges often don't have access to psychological intervention and services. In some cases, judges are not interested in familial history or traumatic childhoods.

What's behind all this misbehavior? Could it be behavior missed? The research and writing of Dr. Bruce Perry have special relevance to understanding children and adolescents who land in the juvenile justice system. Having attended conferences during which Dr. Perry lectured on attachment disorders, trauma, negligence, and abuse, I have followed his website and kept up with his latest research. His essay "Bonding and Attachment in Maltreated Children," one in a series of articles in the ChildTrauma Academy's Parent and Caregiver Education Series, has proven central to my understanding of the residents of Juvenile Hall. His definition of attachment and his assessment of the brief window of opportunity essential for adequate bonding led us to a better understanding of what many of these youths had missed in early childhood.

1)Significant people in your life: myself

a) who brings you into Juvenile Hall? Police

b) who picks you up from Juvenile Hall? foster People

c) who do you love? myself

d) who do you respect? myself & anybody who deserves Respect

e) who do you admire? Jamier Jagr

2)Write us what you remember about these topics and at what age.

a) remember being scared? When I was ten I was affaid of freddy crouger

b) steal something? ever since I was eight I was on my own

c) help a friend? when my best friend got shot I took care of him until the ambulance came

d) question your happiness? havent really ever had something 2 be happy about

3) What is a family? dont Know

4) Has anyone ever called you stupid? If so when, and did you believe him/her?
Yeah and no I didnt believe them

5) Have you ever had a pet? What kind of pet and what do you remember about it?
A rottwieler and what I remember is He acted like a Person

6) Is this your first time in Juvenile Hall? If not, how many times have you been in here?
No I've been here 5 or 6 times and 2 camp once

7) Who do you consider a role model in your life? Why?
Nobody

8) What was your most memorable event in your past?
When my Mom died

9) I live with my:
    a) mother
    b) father
    c) both
    d) other

Bass (boy), age 15

ithis pig are pasted outside
of the hotel, talking about some
body. butt the pigs are
stapid thay thik that thay
cood do nething

Beck (boy), age 15

What is attachment?

...In the field of infant development, attachment refers to a special bond characterized by the unique qualities of the special bond that forms in maternal-infant or primary caregiver-infant relationships. The attachment bond has several key elements: (1) an attachment bond is an enduring emotional relationship with a specific person; (2) the relationship brings safety, comfort, soothing and pleasure; (3) loss or threat of loss of the person evokes intense distress...

What happens if [the] window of opportunity is missed?

...Children without touch, stimulation, and nurturing can literally lose the capacity to form any meaningful relationships for the rest of their lives... There are, however, many millions of children who have some degree of impaired bonding and attachment during early childhood. The problems that result from this can range from mild interpersonal discomfort to profound social and emotional problems. In general, the severity of problems is related to how early in life, how prolonged, and how severe the emotional neglect has been.

—Bruce Perry, M.D., Ph.D

I feel...

i feel really bored and angry. My heart is broken and my life has fallen apart. I wonder how something can repair this wound that lys in my heart. I'm really depressed. Sitting in a room all alone. Everything inside of me is about to explode. I feel miserable. My family members abandoned me. Its hard my friend Shirley left me. And all I have is my sister. No one cares anymore. My mom doesn't come see me regularly like other people's parents. Some of my friends parent visit them everyday, yet mine barely now. I haven't heard from my dad and mom in a long time. I haven't seen my brother in a year, I haven't seen my other brother in months. Life is so depressing. My boyfriends somewhere in an unknown world. I haven't heard from him in a long time. My homies also abandoned me. I no longer have anyone except a couple of friends. I want to change this life around except how... I can't bring a brother back out from the Hall. He's been charged as an adult. Maybe 8 or 9 years until I see him again. Why is my life filled with so much misery? Is there a lesson to be taught more than I've learned? Why? Why! Is this a clue telling me that Cinderalla has or is gonna meet prince charming or is the Prince going to get kissed by the princess? My main concern is why? why is this happening to me? I know I've commited a crime, but

His punishment is way beyond the border lines. I got sentenced to 210 days and now! It seems like I'm getting sentenced with more than the Judge gave me. My main question is why? why is it happening to me? by coincidence or do things happen there are meanings for happening? why? why? why? The time I spend in here is really long yet why so much time. I ran a ged program, but yet I don't get anything for it. I might as well just give up a to bad. I'm a team leader, yet no one listens. They always ignore me. Are they just ignorant people? why? why? Why? Why? Why? Why? Why? why? why me?

Hui (girl), age 15

Having outlined some of the key causes of attachment disorder in young children, Dr. Perry also offers suggestions of what adults can do to help those maltreated as youths and heading for an adult life of alienation and, perhaps, criminality. Two of his 10 suggestions in particular have stayed with me.

Try to understand the behaviors before punishment or consequences:
...When these children hoard food, for example, it should not be viewed as "stealing" but as [the] result of being deprived of food during early childhood. A punitive approach to this problem (and many others) will not help the child mature. Indeed, punishment may actually increase the child's sense of insecurity, distress and need to hoard food. Many of these children's behaviors are confusing and disturbing to caregivers. You can get help from professionals if you find yourself struggling to create or implement a practical and useful approach to these problems...

Be consistent, predictable and repetitive: Maltreated children with attachment problems are very sensitive to changes in schedule, transitions, surprises, chaotic social situations, and, in general, any new situation... Because of this, any efforts that can be made to be consistent, predictable and repetitive will be very important in making these children feel "safe" and secure. When they feel safe and secure they can benefit from the nurturing and enriching emotional and social experiences you provide them. If they are anxious and fearful, they cannot benefit from your nurturing in the same ways.

—Bruce Perry, M.D., Ph.D

Dr. Amy Lansing, a neurobiologist and clinician studying young offenders in San Diego, also believes that children with attachment problems can benefit from nurturing emotional and social experiences even within the juvenile justice system. "People forget these are just kids, after all. Do they commit crimes? Sure. Should they be held accountable? Sure. Does our system work? Not a chance. These are kids who simply want to know and feel love. There is a public perception that these youths are beyond redemption, have no empathy, and can't form attachments. In truth, that perception reflects only a small percentage of youth who are detained and/or incarcerated."

When we talked to her after we ended our visits to the Hall, Lansing offered further hope for resolution of early attachment issues and the potential for young people's continuing growth when she noted that, "We are learning that development in the prefrontal cortex—the part that makes us so 'us,' so human, that is responsible for planning, decision making, and plays a prominent role in social behavior and empathy—extends not only until late adolescence and the early 20s but even until the 30s and 40s."

In the juvenile justice system, it is rarely "too late" to intervene.

I was born on 2,11 at 11:00 am
my dad was not there Just my
mom. my dad was in Jail
moved to san diego when
when I was
3 Year's ould my
mom got Lock up agine

my mom got out she did
drug's a gine

Jones (boy), age 15

5

Timelines of Growth
Absence of Love

If the monkeys have taught us anything it's you've got to learn
to love before you learn how to live.

—**Harry F. Harlow, Ph.D.**, "This Week," March 3, 1961

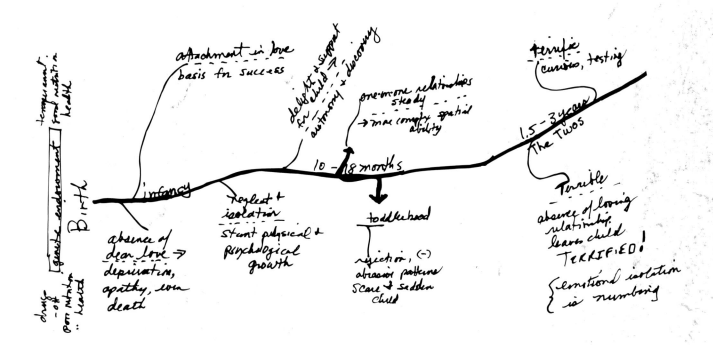

I called upon Dr. Diane Campbell, a practicing psychiatrist board certified in psychiatry and in child-adolescent psychiatry, to personally discuss some of the writings and drawings the kids created for Polly and me in the Hall. I wanted to know, in particular, if any of the youths' contributions during our sessions in Juvenile Hall revealed a lack of the essentials for a good start in life. Dr. Campbell met with us in my office on 20 separate occasions.

In the course of our discussions, Dr. Campbell helped me create a timeline indicating the important growth stages from birth through adulthood; the timeline in its entirety appears on the front and back endpages of this book. "Cool things take place above the center line," she said, referring to the "normal" progress of growth steps we had drawn above the timeline. Below the line we had depicted difficulties and what she called "derailments" or arrested behavior in a neglected or poorly nurtured child. "Crawling, creeping, walking cause excitement... It's interesting to see when patients get stuck at certain times."

Susan: With adults do these things glare at you during therapy sessions?

Diane: Yes. Stages of development are fascinating. The development begins during pregnancy. Everything that happens at one stage effects the sequence of stages to follow. It's not just a simple ra-ta-tat-tat moving forward step by step.

She suggested we begin our discussions by talking about the most serious form of abuse and neglect—isolating a child from birth onward.

Diane: René Spitz, some 60 years ago, studied *hospitalism*. His findings disclose some powerful stuff. First of all, hospitalism is a term that was coined with mothers who gave birth in prison. What's significant is that when babies born in prison got to stay with the mothers, the babies did OK. When they took the babies from the mothers and put them in an institutional setting, there was an enormous amount of disease and death due to anaclitic depression, an *absence of attachment*.

During the first six months, if the mother dies or goes away and you substitute a new mother, human babies do well as long as it's a good second mother. But if there's no new attachment, it's terrible. The baby calls for the mother for a few days, then goes into a kind of whining, then cries instead of calls, and if the mother still doesn't come, and there's no other human attachment, the baby doesn't eat, and then dies. It's very important to replace the primary beloved if that person is removed for whatever reason. Otherwise, the baby is at a huge risk of dying. A huge risk.

Polly: What if your mom disappears after you are two or three years old?

Diane: That's different, because there's more psychological structure. For a two or three-year-old, if there's support—parenting support, family support—and if development has gone well, a huge "if," the child should be OK. There's often severe depression, but it's not usually going to result in death.

Susan: What if there's no firm lasting attachment, and many changes in the environment?

Diane: When we look at violent, depressed people with a series of attachment figures leaving one after another, it's pretty devastating. Still, there are some fascinating, resilient children who thrive in spite of this loss. If a child has had terrible things happen to him but he thrives, we look for "why." We learn as much as we can from him because we can apply that knowledge to help other children. There's a book by a child psychiatrist, E. James Anthony, called *The Resilient Child*. Anthony studied these children and found that with a good first few years of life and a caring adult meaningfully involved, a lot of developmental stuff can remarkably take place in some children. We are a resilient species. The resilient child is able to go from emotional devastation to a safe place.

Susan: It's curious to me how children can relate through their senses and memories.

Diane: Yes. Think of Linus's famous blanket, which made Charles Shultz a gazillion bucks. Beginning around age one you're separated off and on from Mom, if every day she goes to work, you might lug around your blanket or your teddy bear, an object that smells just right to the toddler and usually dreadful to the adult. Don't wash it...you wash it at your peril, or the child's peril, more to the point. It's wonderful the way an object like this will sustain a child through little absences. If the child is going to recover from the temporary loss, this is like a bridge to the absent person. They're called transitional objects because they get you through a transition, where in infancy you're absolutely dependent. They help you in the

To be a daughter

Growing up
    She went through pain
heartbreak, puberty
    and all kinds of change
And right by her side
    there was her mother
showing her love
    like no other
They argued and fought,
    but she didn't understand
Her mother would be there
    to lend her hand
So finally the day came
    and her life took a turn
and when she felt that all failed
    Her mother was there for her
So from that day

Steinley (girl), age 16

transition toward basic inner reliance, forming a psychological structure that is guiding.

Susan: Can children stay at that level—that transitional level—for an indefinite time, into adulthood?

Diane: Yes, they can be stuck there. They can be stuck! You can get stuck at any of the developmental stages, no fault of your own. If you're a little child and too many overwhelming things happen, you drag those issues forward, complicating every other stage of development. To do it massively is emotionally devastating.

Susan: When young people go into Juvenile Hall, they're offered very little in terms of a reason to be able to develop trust.

Diane: Right. And they need a trustworthy someone. If a child is constantly let down in the most basic of ways, abandoned repeatedly by an untrustworthy person, it's almost impossible for that child to grow, and the child never resolves issues. Very painful. That's where we talk about losing a whole generation. A good-enough someone is absolutely required for any kind of life in any kind of community.

Susan: We felt there were several kids in the units with potential.

Polly: They could see our reactions and you know they've seen it somewhere.

Diane: The teenager plus you, and there's a spark. Young people want to be able to share and you presented something real, at last.

Susan: The young girl who was headed off to the CYA prison in Norwalk—very sharp, very engaging.

Diane: Yes, she wrote and wrote. Look at that... "...they argued and fought, but she didn't understand her mother would be there to lend her hand..." She's writing in the third person to keep herself distanced. Her mother was there for her. Then her life took a turn. Oh, she weaves in poetry. "There was her mother who... And her mother..." Isn't that something?

It's hard to understand a youth going off for two years of incarceration and yet able to write this beautifully. That's the rare teenager—one of the ones you want to look for because you can help them. But we need to keep in mind that the real intervention needs to begin in infancy. A good infancy—a loved baby—is essential for any intervention that's going to happen later on in life. If you haven't been a loved baby, you don't have the basics. It's almost impossible to infuse the basics, afterward.

Killing Punks

Bramble (boy), age 17

Susan: A good parent doesn't want to think he's abusive to his child, and yet we use expressions like, "Abuse starts early." Is it important to talk about what abuse starts early?

Diane: How about looking at it as, "The absence of love starts early"? It's not just abuse or violence that causes major disturbances. By simply not having a loving person during infancy, a child is subjected to anaclitic depression. You can take a child away from the mother in prison and put him in a hospital environment, and get him away from quote, "abuse," but if you don't include what babies need—love, eye contact, being held, cuddled, fed, kept clean—then the basics aren't there.

That's where it starts. And without early love, there's nothing to build on, and intervention later on is intensely frustrating—it doesn't work. The caring adult trying to be good to a really messed-up teenager may not understand that there is a group of kids who have gone through a lot of foster parents and have had the experience of several people pushing them away. These kids then try and push the caring person away...the potential parents are so confused. Should they keep this losing kid or send him back?

Susan: In the future, when they haven't been loved, how can they love?

Diane: They don't use words like "love" the same way that a loved person does. They can't. They just say the word. We talk about key phases, achieved in infancy, in the development of what we call *basic trust*. Deciding whether someone is trustworthy or not, whether you can relax in that person's arms and be cuddled. That's basic stuff. Knowing that when you're hungry, as an infant, that you will be fed, that the environment is safe. It is very basic to be loved, to experience cooing, talking, eye contact, lovely things—wonderful moments.

Draw for us a threatening place.
etc.

I can't draw it but I can exsplain it. A threatning place is a place where you were fighting all the time. Where you see fighting all the time. Just a vary violent place

I can tell you my ~~etc.~~ etc. is not varry well becouse I haven't been to school vavry much since 7th grade ~~----~~.

If you were told to create the perfect environment (place to grow up) what would it be like?
Include the following items:
1. education
2. food
3. place to sleep
4. clothes - style
5. other people

It would have the best education in the U.S.A. the house would be big anough to fit my whole family the food wood be great there would be kid in every other house so I could have more friends, dress style would be just like the style today and no vilionce.

Draw for us a space you like to go for 'your time' - a time of peacefulness.

Here

On top of the highest mountin in the world

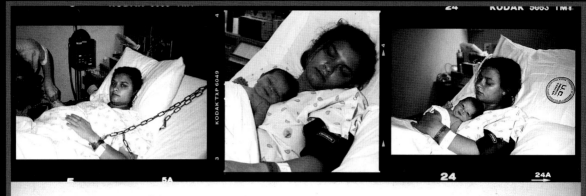

'This picture Really captured my heart Because I have Been trying to have a Baby For So Long and I havent Been able to get pregnant and I wish that I was Able to and it makes me so sad Because I want a baby too! So dose my Boy Friend And weve been trying But it just wasent working and I was wondering is there some thing wrong with me or my partner Because I tryed For three months and it didnt Work! I Really wish that I could Be Looking on in the Same position as that girl Because I want my own Baby too. And She Looks So happy Being able to have her own child. Mayby some-time in the future I will have one.

Touts (girl), age 17

Polly: What percentage of youths in Juvenile Hall would you think were not truly loved?

Diane: I think it's huge. And I think you're saying you can tell the exceptions—the ones who have had basic beginnings. However, the complex individual is the good-looking felon who is charming and has charmed forever and uses the words one wants to hear. There's no conflict within that person. He doesn't know the difference between right and wrong, yet he talks the words. For example, if I were to entertain the idea of murder, I might sit here and think about it, but as I made a plan to murder a particular person I would go, "Wait a minute!" I would never actually murder, and I would never even come close to it. But if someone who does not have a functioning conscience entertains the same ideas, then society better stop him or someone's going to end up dead. See, these people can use the words, "It's wrong to kill," but then they turn around and say, "Hey, in my case, this person pissed me off, so it's OK to kill him." Then he may say, "I won't do it again," but someone else aggravates him, and with no conscience to stop him he kills again.

Polly: How do we develop a conscience?

Diane: Little kids usually go through a stage, around four or five years old, when they want to "kill" their mommy or daddy. They don't do it, of course, but then this stage gets revisited during adolescence. The issues get a second go-around with a different kind of power behind them. When little children say, "I hate you," they really don't feel love at the same time, the way a more mature individual would. They really don't understand that Mom loves them the whole time. Kids in the Hall have similar feelings—anger carried forward from childhood. At times they bang on the wall, kick each other or spit. Many children gradually become people who cannot respond to loving overtures from kind others or to our educational systems. One of the outcomes of that is that they go into illegal groups and activities.

Polly: During adolescence?

Diane: Adolescence is the second separation/individuation. Kids have grown up enough to go out and be more involved with the world, but if the first separation at two didn't occur in a healthy way, issues compound at adolescence. So, how did these kids end up in Juvenile Hall? Their first go-around with separation wasn't loving, and the child's issues got pulled along through the grade-school years, exploding with puberty, and now they're dealing with unsolved early issues, without the psychological structure to keep those issues within bounds, without the social support to give them a grounding and a pathway through adolescence, and they get in quote "trouble" and end up here.

Susan: How do they enter adulthood?

Diane: In many cases, I don't think these people get into adulthood. They are not adults by any understanding I have. No responsibility for their actions, no consequences, no empathy, no right and wrong. Freud said, "Maturity is the capacity to love and to work." These people can't love or work.

Susan: Some children don't trust the love offered to them if there's been an absence of love for years.

Diane: It isn't always an absence, but a conspiracy of events, that makes whatever love someone's trying to give not receivable. This can lead to fury on the part of the giver, and fury on the part of the receiver. It's complicated stuff. The juveniles won't let people get close because they're convinced they'll be hurt, or that the giver of love will go away. In either case, they don't dare take that enormous risk. I think the earlier the abuse or neglect, the worse the outcome. Take mothers who use crack and have babies who are really damaged neurologically—jumpy, easily startled, unable to concentrate and often unable to think. A certain number die in utero. Others can't learn to modulate their own responses because either they're born addicted to crack or they haven't had the attachment experience, haven't been picked up, cuddled, and walked around with, haven't had the bodily contact that seems to be the way to modulate.

From the point of view of vulnerability, an infant born prematurely is more at risk for abuse than a full-term infant. Premature babies are more demanding. They're not as organized, neurologically. A mother often rages at herself and even at the infant, compared to when things go well and she receives wonderful comfort from her baby. Major stuff.

There's got to be a loosening of defenses, letting go of the way you were accustomed to being organized before you were pregnant. The woman who is psychologically healthy enough will relax the strengths she used to rely on. Throughout her pregnancy really work on becoming a new person, in a whole new stage of life.

Susan: Several girls in Juvenile Hall have had babies. They have no concept of being a parent or having a family.

Diane: None whatsoever. They have babies because sex is exciting. On top of that, if you haven't let go of childhood to become a teenager, then you're certainly not an adult. You never feel like your two feet are on the ground. If you get pregnant in all of that? Oh! Then there are several problems with the bonding.

Susan: And especially if they never bonded with their own mothers.

Diane: A lot of people don't have a good, easy relationship with their own mothers. We tend to repress what is upsetting and unfinished so that we can attend to the rest of life. A lot of these girls in the Hall are at a terrible risk if they haven't received the bedrock for solid psychological development—basic trust—in the first several months of life. It's not, "I don't know if I trust you or not." It's almost, "Can I breathe? Can I eat? Is this earth safe? Can I negotiate through problems?" If you don't have basic trust to begin with, there's nothing to build on psychologically.

Susan: Do these children develop resentment?

Diane: I would say they have an over-reliance on very few coping skills, one of which is resentment. They can't give up the resentment because they need it. Most of these vulnerable children, or adults, need to broaden their repertoire and develop more subtle skills. The guy who expresses his anger by punching out the walls, his spouse, or his baby may not know what else to do. He learned hitting as a child and there's no distance between the impulse and the action.

Susan: The juveniles in the Hall express their anger by spitting, hitting.

Diane: Yes. They have nothing else to rely on to help them modulate feelings of anger. They discharge their angry impulses by using their body. When you're a toddler, developmental tasks are required or the issues drag forward. When you're six, you shouldn't still be totally insisting that you rule the roost at home.

A mom hitting her child because she's mad has nothing to do with childrearing. It has to do with anger. So many mothers are vulnerable, and it's not their fault. They've grown up with no access to controlling their own impulses. When they have a two-year-old who makes

Las Colinas Women's Detention Facility – Santee, CA

them feel powerless as a parent they do the only thing they know—they hit to get rid of their mad feelings and let that little baby know how mad they really are.

Susan: When I interviewed women in jail, some of them thought they were acting responsibly by hitting their children. And the kids in Juvenile Hall talk about violence in the home almost as if it's normal.

Diane: You bet. That's why I say it's not their fault. It's ongoing stuff, from generation to generation. How do we stop it? By starting with little children, finding out the child's developmental strengths and vulnerabilities, and then figuring out how to break the cycle. We need to teach specialized parenting, but it's tough. We need to help overwhelmed parents learn how to set limits with their toddlers without expressing fury. Parents feel inadequate. Nothing they do seems to make a dent. Then they feel terrible, vengeful, and some resort to violence. Even parents who have the best of coping skills often feel furious and frustrated, but those parents don't use violence against their child.

Susan: Coaches in the Hall referred to the youths as "willful."

Diane: Buzzwords. If a child is really stubborn and you feel you have to exert force, it may be that the problem has gone inside the child and that the child actually has to work it out. No matter how much you apply force or pressure as a parent or teacher in a child's life, the problem remains because it's gone inside the child. It's not that the child is stubborn. It's that the problem has been going on over a period of years and has a life of its own within the child. That's where psychological treatment has to happen. But *how*, in our society? Therapy is expensive, and even if we had the money, we don't have the trained professionals.

How? That is the question. How can society and its institutions reach inside that unparented child and nurture him or her—appropriately and cost-effectively?

Draw for us a space you like to go for 'your time' - a time of peacefulness.

Waters (boy), age 15

Do you feel your contribution can help kids stay out of trouble? If not, what needs to happen?

Start hitting your kids at a young age.

This lady looks
as if she is
very emotional
and distrate. she looks
like she has tons
of problems
life she seems
as if she needs lots
of care in her.
and she looks
as if she is
coming down
of a crack
cocaine hi it
makes me feel
almost like me and my
mom when we were both
hi and coming down of cocaine
it was the worst time in my
whole life my mother and I in
were so messed up and when
I look at this woman at I
see my whole life and a lost
soul in this young woman
and my conclusion is that
I hop this woman lives
a long life and a healthy one
at that

Cameron (girl), age 14

6

Addiction and Anger
Acting Out

My mom got me on crack. My mom and me did it together. I was selling it first
and then I kept on comin' home with it and she kept wantin' it. I was 13.

—**Cameron** (girl), resident of GRF, Juvenile Hall

Polly and I had established a comfortable pattern of entering and exiting the Hall, visiting the girls in GRF, as well as the individual visitation rooms for one-on-one visits. I had asked the staff how we could meet some of the boys in the Hall. Supervisor Tim told us that would take a different type of organization and set up. It was not customary to pull two or three boys out of a unit for special attention. There were many more boys than girls housed in the Hall and the boys were divided into units based on age, criminal behavior, social and educational development.

By this time, the girls looked forward to our visits. We did not abandon those sessions to meet up with the boys. The boys' units were so structured that we had to set up sessions in advance. The coaches needed to organize the evening for our events, having the boys fed, showered, and understanding they were going to cooperate as a unit for our visits.

Later that night we returned to GRF and met Coach Jan Simpson. This positive and upbeat young coach really understood the girls in the Hall.

> **Susan**: Are the kids reasonably happy in the Hall? Is it a safe place for them?
>
> **Coach Jan**: I don't think any of them are happy. We're not allowed to ask, "How's your home life?" or anything about their crime. If we did, we'd have to write a report, and that's a liability for us if they go to court... "I told Coach..."
>
> All kids like control and don't like being out of control. We offer a structured environment. Most kids follow the rules. It's safe in here. Lots of the parents are abusers or dealers. These kids are children. They want somebody who cares. We care. They interpret it that way.

Coach Jan left and returned to the GRF conference room with Cameron. Sands, out of AR, followed and the girls sat down at opposite ends of the table.

> **Cameron**: I'm really mad because five letters [from her mother] came for me today. I want 'em 'cause they make me feel close to my mom.
> **Susan**: You can write your mom while she's in prison?
> **Cameron**: Yeah. She got sent there for five years. She robbed 13 nursing homes.

Cameron knew she had been sent the letters, yet the Hall wouldn't deliver them to her yet. As in adult jails and prisons, mail is carefully screened in the Hall, and mail from a prison to the Hall in particular would be opened and examined.

this lady looks as if she's frustrated. she looks as if she also thinking of what's going on on the otherside of the fence. she also looks as if she had been crying because she has dark circles under her eyes and it looks as if her eyeliner is now smeared. she also looks as if she has alot of hate and anger in her eyes by the expression on her face. I think that im also saying this is because I know what its like to be behind a fence like that and not being able to leave. I wonder if she ever thought the way I do when shes locked up. alls I can do is think of going home and re-thinking of the thing I did to get in here and I think why did I do that? I was so stupid? I keep wishing why cant I just rewind the whole thing? do it all over again and I wouldn't be here? I wonder if she wishes she could do the same. just rewind it back so it wouldn't come to the point of doing what we did to get locked up. I wonder if she regrets doing what she did. because I know that I did. and I hope that I never have to go to the point of ending up where she is right now?

Las Colinas Women's Detention Facility – Santee, CA

Sands (girl), age 16

Polly: Sands, do you have any relatives who've been in prison?

Sands: Oh yeah. My brother and my dad and all my uncles. My dad's supposed to be getting out this year. He's been in four or five years. I haven't seen him at all. I think it's better for me 'cause he's a big-time drug user and I like using certain drugs and he would give them to me.

The girls now changed the subject to drug use. It was striking how naturally they made the connection between drugs and prison, yet in many cases they were on their way to the same lifestyle as their drug-using parents. These kids knew they were likely to end up in prison.

Polly: Cameron, you used drugs, right?

Cameron: Crack. My mom got me on it. My mom and me did it together. I was selling it first and then I kept on comin' home with it and she kept wantin' it. I was 13, 14.

Polly: Weren't you scared carrying it around and dealing?

Cameron: I'd rather do that than prostitute.

Susan: What does it mean to you to give your body up to a man for money?

Cameron: I did it for the reason, uh… Well, my family is a little messed up, and I didn't think any of them really wanted me or cared for me. This guy was telling me he loved me. When somebody tells you they love you, who are you going to go to? I'm very naive. Without realizing it.

Polly: Sands, is it hard for you to relate to someone like Cameron talking about prostitution?

Sands: Yes. Because I never did it and I never will!

Cameron: This is a stage in my life because I don't even like doing it and I'm not gonna stay doin' it. Some have their stage of smokin' weed… Well, my stage was sellin' drugs, doin' drugs, prostituting. I grew up really fast. I smoked weed since I was 12. My friends got me into it and selling.

Susan: What kind of message do you have for kids out there, 11 or 12?

Cameron: Be a kid and go through school. Stay away from drugs.

Polly: What about your dad?

Cameron: I don't know where he is. He's an alcoholic, too. He just took off. Told me he was going on a business trip and he never came back.

Susan: Was that about the time you started the prostitution?

Cameron: Yeah. It was two summers ago my dad left. Last summer I started prostituting.

Polly: What does it mean for you girls to have a dad?

Sands: Nothin'. A lot of my friends' dads are locked up, too, so I don't know. I'm glad that my stepdad's not here in town. I'm also glad that my real dad is gone in prison.

Cameron: It was, "Don't let your dad find out" or I'd be in trouble. He'd spank me. He grabbed me by the arms…'cause I was a little brat, but some things were uncalled for like one night after he moved to Seattle, he came back and kidnapped me and my little brother away from my mom for three years.

Susan: Did he kidnap you to protect you from your mom?

Cameron: My mom told me he kidnapped us because he was mean but I'm realizing that he took us for our safety. This was in third grade. In fifth grade, in Seattle, I was sitting in the class, doing my schoolwork, when the principal and a detective came in and took me to the office where my mom was standing. She hugged me. I was so happy. I didn't think I'd ever see her again.

Polly: Sands, you have trouble in school?

Sands: No. I started having trouble because of my stepdad. I'd get mad and my mom would argue with me. I really don't like anybody—I don't care who it is—talking to me that way. I get set off real easy.

Cameron: I say something wrong to Sands or just look at her wrong and she's just like...!

Sands: [Laughs] I jus' snap. I remember always saying I will never hit my mom. 'Cause my friends used to hit their moms and I'd say, "How could you disrespect your mom like that!" I don't know what happened. I had so much anger built up that I couldn't take any more. Then she said something—we got in an argument—and I just snapped. I reached out and hit her and after that day—I just kept on hitting her. Both of us were fist fighting. Since then I hit my mom a lot—a lot. I'd push and *smack* her.

Susan: Why did your mom tolerate that?

Sands: She hit me too! We hit each other. It was mutual.

Polly: What do you think would've helped you at that time with frustration and growing up?

Sands: I don't know. I was so out of control. She couldn't have stopped me if she tried.

Susan: Because you were on drugs when you were acting out?

Sands: Yeah. I've done so many drugs I don't remember.

After talking to Diane Campbell, I could see how a lack of basic trust set these behaviors into motion and created a pattern most difficult to reverse without proper therapy and support.

Susan: When do you think the aggressive behavior started?

Sands: Mine started at 12.

Cameron: I was 11 years old, in fifth grade. My mom got physical with me. She's big, too, 5'10". Shorter than me, though. She'd come up and whale at me—*pow, pow, pow*—'cause I have a mouth on me and she's got the anger coming after me. I'd raise a hand to her but she said if I ever raise a hand to her again she'd beat the livin' hell out of me. She'd yell, "You f'ing B-I-T-C-H," and I started callin' her things back. Then she'd come running after me. One time she came after me when I was on the bed. I said, "'F' you, you 'f'ing' whore." And she jumped me and beat me up. I'm not gonna allow my mom to beat me up.

Cameron's story kicked off memories in Sands, and provoked feelings, first of shame, and then guilt over the ways in which Sands treated her own mother. This kind of give-and-take was becoming more common the longer we spent time with the girls.

Sands: I regret ever saying anything like that to my mom or ever putting a hand on her. At the time, I told her she deserved it. I used to warn her, "Get out of my face, 'cause I feel like I'm gonna hit you," but she just stayed in my face and kept on flappin' her mouth and when she got too close to me I reached out and hit her.

I was born and raised to fight. My first fight was when I was five years old. A girl had kicked me when I was laughing at her and then ever since then I been fighting a lot. My mom saw the girl hit me first. My stepdad told me to hit that person. He's always told me to hit back. I'm glad that I know how to defend myself. I do have the confidence right now. He taught me how to fight.

Cameron: Teenagers like us think we know everything.

Sands: I have to have an attitude because these girls are very pushy. "Go get that for me..." [snaps fingers]. They don't even say please. I turn around and go, "Excuse me?"

"When I am upset..."

I   fight

I   HATE

I   have fights

I   get hi

I   throw punshes

I   worrie

I   ~~TAG ON Everything~~

I   yell

I   sleep

I   get aggressive

I   Smoke marijouna

I   Smoke Blunts.

I   ~~coff~~ cry or worry

I   listen to music
or Play the PlayStedion

I   hurt

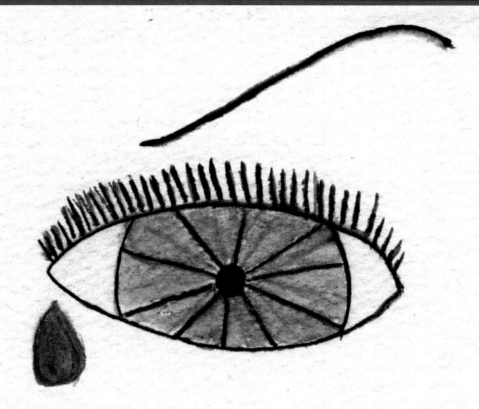

Sands (girl), age 16

7

Getting Stuck
Shamed, Abused, Not Safe

In disorganized families, the child's ability to be curious and feel safe doesn't develop.
The shy or humiliated little boy who can sit and be compliant is doing so for the wrong
reasons—because he's scared, not because he's patient—and his fear keeps him
from learning the interesting things the others are learning.

—**Diane Campbell,** M.D.

The girls spoke openly and frankly. Yet it felt as if we were talking to 40-year-olds one minute and the next minute as if we were talking to conflicted little girls who missed their mothers. During those times a tremendous sadness dominated the mood, replacing mere bravado.

Dr. Diane Campbell returned to my office. We revisited her timeline and we talked about the importance of developing conscience early on, the unfortunate use of "shame on you," and how that affects a child's growth.

> **Susan**: What about shame and guilt?
>
> **Diane**: "Shame on you." Shame comes from the outside, and guilt comes from the inside. Guilt is more complex. When a mother says to a two-year-old, "Shame on you! Go to your room," shame is heaped on the child. You can't heap guilt; it happens on its own. When a little child says at bedtime, "Mommy, I have to tell you something," it's clearly a sign he's working on the development of conscience. Conscience can be pretty harsh early on. It becomes more subtle, more of a guide, only if it's developing well. Remember Jiminy Cricket, Pinocchio's conscience? "Let your conscience be your guide." Let it be your guide, as opposed to your punisher or jailer. When that little preschooler, or the kindergartner, is overwhelmed with guilt at bedtime and says, "Mommy I have to tell you something. I took a cookie. I took a cookie and I ate it," the mother's response is crucial. If she acts as a guide, if she's clear about right and wrong, but is also loving, then the child goes to sleep feeling comforted.
>
> The very stressed-out mother might find herself yelling, "Shame on you, you just messed in your pants again!" Horrible stuff starts up. Resentment builds inside the child who thinks, "Mommy says I'm bad." Pretty soon he says it to himself.
>
> Developing a healthy and appropriate sense of guilt is an important task of early childhood. Shame is from the outside, and many people in our country use the phrase, "Shame on you." Or they'll say, "Bad!"
>
> **Polly**: What's the right thing to do?
>
> **Diane**: You can say it's a "No no," but "Shame on you" is crushing. The toddler hanging over the infant, ready to poke his eye, and mother says, "No no," he pulls his finger away. The

Questionnaire: RC
boys night 1

Packet Number: 9

Initials:
Unit: 900
Age: 15

Is this your first time being in Juvenile Hall? If not, how many times have you been there?

no / 5

a) **Is Juvenile Hall like you thought it would be? Why/why not?**

Yeah, It sucks.

b) **When you get out of Juvenile Hall what would you like to accomplish for other young people so they don't have to experience Juvenile Hall?**

They need to learn the hard way.

Do you think after your release, you'll come back if not, what will you do to make sure you won't return? I know I'll either come back or end up dead.

Are you in school? If not do you have any plans to go back and finish?

no

What have you given deep thought to since you have been in Juvenile Hall?

How not to get caught

If you have one wish to change something in your life, what would it be?

To have a family.

Have you ever been subjected to peer pressure? If so, how did it make you feel? How would you change it if you could and why?

It made me wanna do it.

What was your most memorable event (in your past)?

Getting in a car accident

Do you feel your contribution can help kids stay out of trouble? If not, what needs to happen? Start hitting your kids at a young age.

I am a young person scared about the future. I am scared that

I might have responsibilities.

Yale (boy), age 15

I want Freedom

I hope that I get what I want.

I feel like I'll never make it.

I Beat on things when I am upset.

I wish I could be alone and find some peace and quiet. If I could then everything would be all right. Then I would die there.

I have some brothers and sisters.

Circle one and explain to us why.

I (like/dislike) school? Too much control + responsibility

I (like/dislike) my siblings. ⟩ They don't want me.

I (like/dislike) family members.

I wish at times that I could live alone. (T/F)

I wish at times someone would understand me. That person would be close to me.

I feel education is shit .

If I could share something important with you I would tell you
Take care of your kids cause it sucks when no one cares.

I used to burn crickets and grasshoppers. I used to get my dog and my friends cat High. I shaved a cat once.

> Juvenile misconduct is increasing due to forces we all understand—guns and drugs. At the same time, the amount of money being spent on kids is being reduced. So that means more kids will commit more serious acts and end up in non-rehabilitative confinement.
>
> –Bill Boyland, *former Chief Deputy Public Defender*

impulse to poke is there and the prohibition from mom is there, "No no." The ones who get their hands slapped will slap their own hands. They do what was done to them. The mother goes, "No no," the toddler takes the hand away, mother says, "Good boy. Oh, so good!" That toddler is getting the sense of being loved while learning what is a "No no."

The two-year-old who goes to poke the baby sister's eye, and then he gets yelled or screamed at, and told "Shame on you," will cringe. The mother abandons the two-year-old and scoops up the baby and goes away, leaving the two-year-old by himself. That's damaging. That really doesn't help develop the psychological structure that's going to be the resilient child.

Susan: What about the other side of the coin, a dad who doesn't want his son to "wuss out"?

Diane: "I want you to be able to handle yourself like I do." A little boy copies his dad but the parent has to give the child tasks that work for a child. It's really tricky to know how best to help a child respond to a bully without resorting to bully tactics. There are good reasons why responsible parents don't put guns in the hands of children.

Or a dad will say to his daughter, "There's only one thing guys want," and that kind of talk leads a girl to feel scared and confused. She has no idea how to respond to sexual overtures from a boy and the parents don't know how to guide her. Vulnerable parents, vulnerable children. It's a constant weave of life.

Most of us know how dangerous it is to give a gun to a young boy. That's not how we teach young children to protect themselves. But some parents do those things. They give guns to young kids.

Susan: I saw so many inconsistencies when I was interviewing in the women's facility. The inmates appeared mentally disorganized. They spoke of feeling guilt while locked away from their kids. "How do you think I feel being away from my kids?"

Diane: They may not be feeling guilty. They may not be capable of feeling real guilt. Or they may feel guilty, but it may overwhelm them and they haven't learned to modulate it.

Susan: So, as mothers these women have unfinished business from age five, a stage where a healthy child starts to develop guilt.

Diane: The term we use is developmental *arrest*. You see them stuck and grappling with the same problem over and over.

Susan: "Am I loved or am I not loved?" It's ironic that arrested behavior gets people arrested later in life.

Polly: What about the sexually abused child? Is it worse than physical abuse?

Diane: Sexual assault is both physical and intimate. An excellent book on the subject is *Soul Murder* by Leonard Shengold, a psychoanalyst. Abuse seeps into every corner of the mind. Huge numbers of women have been sexually abused, a very personal kind of sexual assault.

It's such an intimate action and you can't effectively fight back. When the victim is a child, and the perpetrator is someone who's supposed to be protective of the child, then the confusion is awful.

Polly: How does thrill-seeking—seeking out roller coasters—relate to juveniles in the Hall?

Diane: Kids are drawn to different sorts of roller coasters. For some, it's like a sexual high, or a drug high. For others, it's an escape; it's fun, a literal roller coaster, the thrill in the arms of "safety," an extension of being tossed up in the air and knowing Daddy's going to catch you. Some over-controlled people get a thrill out of letting go of their control.

Regarding sex, one of the critical developmental steps is moving into what we still call the Oedipal age, the imaginative flowering of the four-year-old. If a child develops normally, most of the earlier issues have been pretty well handled. But a child in the four-year-old preschool room, or kindergarten room, stands out like a sore thumb if he's still throwing tantrums over and over. And it's upsetting to the other kids, who are still somewhat fragile.

Susan: You've mentioned how crucial a step it is, going from being a two-year-old to a four-year-old.

Diane: Absolutely. The child who stays stuck at the age of two grows up to be one of the people we all know who can only think of himself. He has to be self-centered, because if he doesn't focus on himself he's afraid he'll fall apart. This sort of person maintains control by throwing various sorts of tantrums, sometimes at an international level. He may run a corporation, but he'll do it through intimidation and control. These people are bullies, a result of not having grown through a bedrock stage of development. They have a terrible time parenting.

The child who turns three or four and hasn't left behind his two-year-old control issues—who's still pooping in his pants, throwing tantrums to get his way, grabbing toys, not able to have fun playing with other children—that child is very much at risk. That's why most preschools have room divisions for the two-year-old and the four-year-old.

> I realy don't Remember my chidhood because I've tered so hard to block it out. The earliest memary I have is at the age of 11 when I was malested by my grandfather.

Brown (girl), age 16

First memory you ever had.

Dob.

My first memory is when I was four and my uncle broke my arm that is a memory I will never forget another one is my pet baby bird. barney I loved that bird I used to sleep with it. It used to sleep on my pillow she used to eat my popcorn I used to feed it rice too! but then one day my step-father accidently smothered my bird. I cried a long time but I have a picture of my birds big head and I don't let anyone touch it.

always♥

My First Memory

I remember when I was 5 and I started kindergarden and my mom tried to leave me, I wouldn't let her leg go. She tried to pull me off with her hands so I bit her. So she grabbed my mouth and tried to pull me off so I ran out and got in my car so my mom agrued with the teacher to let her stay so my mom stayed a week with me and I was able to go to school without her then. My mom was so proud of me, we had a party at my class.

We shared more of the writings from Juvenile Hall with Diane.

Diane: Some of the handwriting is amazing. Teenagers don't have mental or emotional stability, and the handwriting reflects that. And what a great statement from one of your coaches: "It stresses me how girls go through puberty. They try things they aren't ready for."

Susan: The youths in the Hall talked about horrific fights, drinking brawls in the home, and even drugs.

Diane: We call adults who are stuck in two-year-old issues *borderline personalities*. They have a character pathology, meaning it's sustained. They're stuck with it. It's very hard to treat. They love you as long as you're perfect. They can't handle any kind of frustration in any relationship. A lot of people have borderline features, but it's not their total personality organization. They struggle as adults, but were able to develop a conscience back in those early crucial years.

Another crucial period comes at about age six-and-a-half. Vibrant, colorful times, little boys playing with swords. They do these things to work out the issues of their age.

Susan: The first memory, does it reflect on developmental issues?

Diane: We need to stay in touch with what these teenagers are trying to show us about themselves. The girl who said she couldn't remember anything—I bet the memory was so awful she had to block it out. And the girl whose first memory was being molested. Heartbreaking. First memories generally have a hazy quality to them; we call them screen memories—like looking through a veil.

Kindergarten is a transitional year. In first grade, we expect kids to sit in a classroom and direct attention outwardly and learn. Some boys are kept back a year. It just takes them a little longer to get through the excitable Oedipal period, when they want to be playing with swords all the time, or out on the jungle gym. That's why we have recess, to work off the steam. It's why good first-grade teachers have exercises for the children to do during class. In order to read, children need a healthy sense of curiosity. For kids too scared to be curious, they don't learn to read.

Susan: Stats are out that 43 percent of fourth graders cannot read.

Diane: In disorganized families, the child's ability to be curious and feel safe doesn't develop. The shy or humiliated little boy who can sit and be compliant is doing so for the wrong reasons—because he's scared, not because he's patient—and his fear keeps him from learning the interesting things the others are learning. That little boy, in order to learn to read, needs to make the same mistakes the other children do, but he doesn't dare. He misses out on the normal trial and error of growing up. Kids in healthy families often learn to read before they go to school, and it's not always a matter of IQ. Some average-IQ kids start school knowing how to read. Reading is exciting to them.

Polly: A lot of parents don't read to their kids.

Diane: That's right. "It's a wonderful book, come into my lap and I'll read it to you." Again, excitement within safety—and without the roller coaster—doesn't happen for many children. Instead they are exposed to violence within their home both from the media and from the teenagers and adults around them.

Susan: The sword age carried forward?

Diane: Yes. The child who says to another child, "Hey, you can handle this," and forces the other child to sit through a slasher flick—that's not playing. The child is being assaulted visually and emotionally. Or maybe he's told by a parent, "Sit and watch this flick. I gotta go and get a beer." This same Dad may slap Mom around every night and get drunk. Frequently when parents say, "He can handle it, he'll be fine," they misjudge—it's too much for the child, frightens the child. If they do this over and over, then the relationship is at risk. How can the child trust an adult who says you're fine and then submits the child to violence?

A lot of teachers love to teach fourth grade. They love to see kids soak up information. If development has proceeded fairly normally, fourth-graders have learned basic trust. They've gained a sense of the autonomy of their own bodies and the limits of their own power. They're done with the two-year-old tantrums, have moved through the three- to five-year-old stage and had a flowering of imagination and fantasy life and learned cooperativeness at play. They've developed a pretty workable conscience that's not overly punishing, and they can concentrate on the outside world because the inner world is not as scary as it was around the age of five when nightmares are normal. When you leave all that behind and become the teachable school-age child, you're doing pretty well. That's why teachers love fourth grade.

Susan: But play is so different these days with video games, organized sports and competitions. Kids' imaginations can't fully develop with today's tools.

Diane: That's true. They aren't out playing and creating on their own. They may be creating in their heads, but they aren't out there with other kids. You don't learn to share power by watching interactions on television. TV may stimulate your imagination, but there's no give and take. What we mean when we say the "teachable school-age child" isn't just a matter of school. Teachable children can focus on learning about the outer world.

Susan: I would like to know how many parents know if their children are healthy.

Diane: That's what I want to do—teach this to parents.

Everything a person is and everything he knows resides in the tangled thicket of his intertwined neurons. These fateful, tiny bridges number in the quadrillions, but they spring from just two sources: DNA and daily life.

–Thomas Lewis, M.D.; Fari Amini, M.D.; Richard Lannon, M.D.
A General Theory of Love

when I think of puberty I think of feelings and emotion and hormonal differences physical I would say that your voice changes like gets deeper and you get hair in odd places and emotional you become a little bit cranky and have mood swings

Cameron (girl), age 14

Puberty
Disrupted from Within

> Imagine the girl developing breasts and having her first period
> when she has never felt solid as a child.
>
> —**Diane Campbell,** M.D.

One of the very concerning issues for these youths was missing out on being teenagers. They seemed to skip stages, moving from being angry children into premature adulthood. Already experiencing lockup, it was as though high school, social growth, and moral accountability were not options for these kids. They took a leap from puberty into adulthood without the tools to carry on successfully.

Polly and I wanted to talk to the girls and see if they grasped the meaning of puberty. To prepare, we decided to have another chat with Dr. Diane Campbell about the subject. She spoke with us about the crucial, disruptive period that begins at puberty. She explained that puberty in today's girls can begin as early as age eight or nine. "When puberty hits, the constructive years of the teachable school-age child are finished. Puberty is disruptive," she said. "The first period generally occurs two years after the budding of the breasts. When puberty hormonally hits, the best preparation for it is the knowledge that you're a good, strong, capable, loved child. Imagine the girl developing breasts and having her first period when she has never felt solid as a child."

During our tenth visit to the Hall, we set out writing and art tools. Each of the girls could choose what they wanted to do for the evening. There were 50 choices of images on cards to write about, or they could make up their own story. We had a new topic each week. This night, after they saw the art supplies and heard they could write on "puberty," the girls wanted to work before dinner.

Cameron, Sands, and Hui behaved like three good kids, attentive and happy, grappling at the center of the table for pens and Conté crayons. I'd have given anything to have been allowed to have my camera to capture their eyes. Cameron's hair was in a ponytail. Sands wore a French braid. Hui, long hair tied back loosely. Each of them, faces unusual and distinct—very pretty girls.

Sands: What music do you have for us tonight?

Polly put on the soundtrack from *The English Patient*. Great reactions. They looked at each other as though we had turned on Mozart.

Hui: The rest of our unit knew we wanted to see you guys.

Hui was very satisfied with herself and with us that night. She smiled as she started to write about puberty. Cameron muttered something about having been "real pissed" earlier that day.

Cameron: I was in group and I threw a desk across the room.

Polly looked aghast.

Polly: You threw a desk? A classroom desk?
Cameron: Yip.
Hui: You shoulda seen her. Yes. I think it was kinda rude for other people in the other group 'cause they were making fun of her.
Sands: And they shut up when you threw the desk, huh? *[All laugh.]* It takes that much? You do something like that to shut them up? Boy, when I get mad they don't do nothin' either.
Cameron: No. It wasn't that. It was just because a lot of anger was built up with this girl and me. It was either me getting AR'd or me kicking the door.

Polly: What's AR'd?
Sands: Administrative removal. When do we get our puberty paper?

Susan: It's right in front of you. Hui's already writing about it.

It was quiet as they wrote. The music helped set the mood. A nice moment. The windows were open. An owl hooted outside the conference room. It hooted again in the evening light as French horns played in the background to Ella Fitzgerald singing, "Heaven, I'm in heaven..."

Cameron: Ha, sounds like my grandma's house. *[She turns up the music.]* My uncle had a wreck, going 100 miles an hour down a boulevard and broke every bone in his face.
Susan: The uncle you thought took the St. Christopher medal from your grandmother?

Cameron had told us, during a previous visit, about this uncle.

Cameron: Yes, probably for drug money.

The girls finished up their writing and we went with them to the cafeteria.

Sands: *[Whining]* I don't know what puberty is.
Hui: You don't have to eat that fast, gosh.
Cameron: Will you bring back Tabasco sauce?
Sands: We're not allowed to bring it back here.
Hui: Puberty is when a girl becomes a woman, where she starts her period, at the age... I think 12 to 18.
Sands: My medicines don't make me hungry.
Cameron: You just go take your medicine.
Sands: No. The doctor increased it.
Cameron: You going to eat your roll?
Sands: You can have it if you want.

Susan: If I ate the way you do I'd be three times your size.
Cameron: You guys aren't locked up. I'm not this fat on the outs.

Cameron pulled out her mail.

Cameron: That's my mom's letter. You want to hear the letter?
Sands: Are you going to cry? I could tell because you're like...

Cameron paused. Then started reading.

Puberty:
How do the changes in your body make you feel?
Who do you talk to when you're confused or just need
someone to talk to?

I think puberty makes me very depressed because when its the time of the month or everyday, all I can do is just stress about problems throughout my whole entire life. I get really aggressive, And I really dislike it! I have to try really hard to hold my temper in, but sometimes. it just happens. It just explodes and makes me really depressed looking back at my past and angry about towards myself on how I treated my family and abused them. It makes me feel guilty. I talk to myself really which really help, but sometimes I talk to a peer cons counselor. to rea release my angry, depression, and temper.

Hui (girl), age 15

Cameron: "I love you...everywhere I go I miss you too, Sweetie. But this shall pass and we will be united in love and faith."

Hui: How sweet. I'm happy for you, Cameron.

Cameron: "Just pray, Cameron. Ask God for help." *[Crying]* "He's helped me. I prayed for you to get off the streets, you may not like what happened but if you were still running out there it might have killed you. I wish I had a phone to tell you how much I love you..." *[Crying]* "but we both know how we feel. Mother's Day is May 11th. I haven't always been the best mom and you have been a handful, too. So my actions... I still do love you, I do, I just got our lives all messed up. Drugs as you know mess up a lot of hearts. Just know we'll never go back. Reach for the stars and do your best and pray because God will take care of the rest. I promise you that I'm going to try and send you a few bucks for your birthday. I know..." *[Crying]* "I know it's coming soon and I'll be there in your heart."

     I miss her.

Susan: Were you that close to dying? *[She nods.]* On the street?

Cameron: No, drugs. Cocaine.

Polly: How long?

Cameron: Long time. "...Don't ever forget I love you with all my heart and soul."

A pause. The music continued in the background. The girls had written, drawn, eaten dinner, talked openly, and shown respect for one another.

Polly: I'm glad she wrote you this letter. How do you feel now?

Cameron: Good. I haven't talked to her since a month before Christmas. Five months ago. The day she dropped me off at the bus station. I was coming down here to do other things bad. That was the day she got arrested.

Susan: She dropped you off thinking you were coming here for what?

Cameron: That I was coming down to hang out for a while with my boyfriend. Only he was really my pimp.

Polly: How old are you?

Cameron: Fifteen.

Leaving GRF we headed down the hallway to the private interview rooms with a coach escort and youth Pendleton. Several kids recognized Pendleton and tried to get her attention by yelling and knocking on their cell doors. The coach closed us in the interview room closest to the control station.

Pendleton: I didn't go to school today because I'm on KP.

She handed us the puberty paper.

Pendleton: I can really start to pick out people going through it. I've witnessed stuff. It seems like to me, as soon as people reach puberty, bam, you know, it's "I'm an adult," ooh. They don't have the mental or emotional stability to do things even though they might have the body. Puberty to most kids is like an excuse to do things.

Polly: How long do you think puberty goes on for?

Pendleton: 'Til you're grown up. I mean like I'm still growing up and maturing. I remember adolescence because I experienced it more than my friends did. My friends were still in their training bras and I was wearing B-cup bras. I hated it. Yeah, I was one of those girls

Puberty

The first thing that comes to my mind when I think of puberty is growing up.

I remember when I was twelve, my friends and I couldn't wait to reach thirteen, because to us, it seemed so old. Everything really started at the teens: make-up, boyfriends, kissing (and other things), more privelages, your period (which for some reason everyone wanted until they finally got it), and curves. (Some of us, though, never get the last one.)

And that was true to me. I was always the ugly, fat, duckling until my 13th. After that, over the next couple months, it changed: my face suddenly always had make-up on, the fat on my stomach disapeered and went elsewhere unto my thighs & hips (ugh.) and, my chest.

And people noticed this, too. Oh, boy, did they notice; by the time the spring came, I was used to people "admiring" my assets. (Even my best guy friend once told me the reason why he loved hugging me was because I was, uh, soft and comfortable. Pig!)

It was suprising, yet flattering. I had guys asking me for my number left & right, when just the year before I couldn't even make them take the first three digits.

Puberty is a great thing; it means you're becoming a woman. The problem is, some girls take puberty as an excuse to grow up to fast.

I know some 14 year old girls who are trying to get pregnate just because their 20-something year old boyfriends are ready. Two years ago they were playing with barbies, and now they think, even though they can barely take care of themselves, that they can have a baby?

And some 14-15 year olds look 5-10 years older; that doesn't mean they have the mentality or emotional stability.

And uh, if their way older boyfriends were worth anything, they wouldn't have anything to do with a <u>girl</u>, and I mean <u>girl</u>, that young.

It destresses me how girls use puberty as an excuse to try things they aren't ready for. Even though your mother might dry a tear of joy because "her baby's becoming a woman" at your first period doesn't mean her baby is a woman yet, nor does she have to act like one.

Puberty is an experience between childhood & being an adult. Don't make that mistake & grow up too fast; once your childhood's gone, you can't get it back.

Pendleton (girl), age 16, page 3

that didn't want her period until 17. I didn't want a chest, hips. I didn't start puberty 'til I was like 13, but by 14... I was in Chula Vista and I had run away. I had no makeup on and I was wearing a little Gucci shirt and pants and this guy was hitting on me and he said he was 21, but he looked like he was 30. I'm all, "I said I'm only 14." He said, "Girl, you wouldn't try to lie to me?" It's weird how I look so much older. I went from this big old fat ugly duckling when my dad would always say, "I can't believe you're so fat. Why don't you lose weight?"

Polly: What kinds of things provoke you?

Pendleton: I just don't understand why people can't be themselves. It gets on my nerves. They're fake. Take guys. I don't think highly of the male species. I honestly don't believe in love. I believe you can love someone, but I don't believe you can be in love. I believe everything gets taken away. Everything changes. It doesn't stay the same. I contradict myself 'cause I'm probably a romantic at heart.

Polly: How's your mom handle what's happening to you?

Pendleton: I don't know. Everyone says my mom is part of an experience. I'm one of those kids whose mom is worse than her kid. She's like, "Oh you totally try to mess me up."

Susan: You said you get to a place where you feel you just have to run. What happens to you at that time?

Pendleton: The reason I run away from home is problems with my mom that I know aren't going to get better. I don't even try to bother with it. It affects the way I feel. The street isn't the best thing for me, but I survive.

Susan: You need an education.

Pendleton: That's what the judge said. That's one reason I'm in here, 'cause he said my IQ is 126. He thought I need to go to school but my PO doesn't want me to go to public school 'cause of the drugs and he said to the court, "She's gonna do drugs again." If I want to be responsible, I will. They probably want to lock me up somewhere where you can't have any phone calls, like the Phoenix House.

Polly: They gave you the MMPI test?

Pendleton: First they gave me an IQ test. He would say, "Do this," and then "Woodie, woodie woo." So I did that. He's all, "You're really scoring them all." I go, "Yes." He pulled out all these little ink things and said, "Tell me what you see." I kept looking at them and all I could see was like ugly bugs. He'd be like, "What is this?" I'd go, "Ugly bug," and he goes like, "Are you playing with me?" I go, "No, that's what I see." He kept saying, "Do you do this? How many sexual partners have you had? What drugs are you taking? Are you taking Ecstasy?" I said, "No." He said, "Don't lie." He doesn't believe me. He was rude. That guy was weird. He was like, "What did you do when you ran away?" I was all, "I hustled." "Did you prostitute? Did you steal?" I'm all, "No." "Well, who did you hustle?" He's all, "Did you do it for sex?" I'm all, "No!" He was just getting on my nerves, the intimidation. That does not work with me. Cops...that's why I hate cops, they try to intimidate you. They try to act all tough and stuff.

Susan: Tell me about the hustling. Is that how you maintained your habit with drugs on the streets?

Pendleton: Yeah, pretty much. I was more of a con artist.

Susan: What do you see yourself doing 20 years down the road?

Pendleton: Probably college. I want to work with kids. *[She takes a piece of the art charcoal and starts to draw a girl's face.]* I think consistency is good. If you're there for kids it'll be so much better. But when it comes down to it, there's always a choice.

Polly: What did you like to do when you were 10 years old?

Pendleton: I played with my dolls.

Susan: Is it hard to live in the same room with three other girls?
Pendleton: Yeah, sometimes when they're asleep. I don't sleep well, especially in here. I consider myself an insomniac. Sometimes I don't go to sleep until an hour or two later. I just think about things.
Susan: What would your mother say to you now?
Pendleton: She'd just say, "If you hadn't been so out of control." "Stick it out!" I love my mom but she's an island. I have my problems and she has something to do with it.

Polly: Would she go into counseling with you?
Pendleton: She started it. We have different tastes. She says I have total control over her and, "I just feel so bad. I don't know what to do with her...a child, I love her but..." She hears me but she doesn't listen.
Polly: When somebody tells you that you're emotionally disturbed...
Pendleton: I just look at him. Come on, I guess I've had problems. I'm not delirious. I've had emotional problems but I'm not disturbed. My mom told me that the psychologist told me I had *severe* problems. I read the report and it was not exactly flattering. It said that I was in denial about my drug problem. I've had my experiences and made mistakes. I wanted the easiest way.

I talked to Diane about the recurring theme I heard from the youths in the Hall—mother or father as supposed protector but also abuser. Polly and I learned a great deal from seeing these young girls and then having a chance to process what we saw in talks with Diane.

Susan: When the protector becomes the abuser, does that have something to do with this pain-pleasure area?

Diane: Yes. Nothing creates more confusion and shame than trying to sort out the abuser-

---

Do you have any family members that have been, or are in jail or prison?

MY DAD WAS IN JAIL.

What are your plans for the future?

GRADUATE AND RAISE MY KID.

What have you given deep thought to since you have been in Juvenile Hall?

MY GIRL THATS RAISING MY KID WITHOUT ME WHILE IM IN HERE

If you have one wish to change something in your life, what would it be?

THE DRUGS AND THE CRIMES IVE COMMITED

Remember when you used to dream as a small child. What did you want to be when you grew up? I USE TO WANT TO BE JUST LIKE MY DAD,

Have you ever been subjected to peer pressure? If so, how did it make you feel? How would you change it if you could and why? YES, I DID DRUGS TO FEEL GOOD AND I WISH I NEVER DID.

Moore (boy), age 16

---

protector. It's so hard to separate, and the infliction of pain from others can lead to the infliction of pain on yourself, since you're both the giver and receiver of what goes on in your own psyche.

Susan: You're a pivotal person in your own life.

Polly: Like harming yourself, mutilation.

Diane: Very much in vogue with teenage girls. Doesn't necessarily imply the diagnostic horror that it used to.

Polly: If you have a mellow child and a chaotic mom and dad, it conflicts with the natural temperament of the child and creates...

Diane: Havoc. Look at it the other way around, too. If calm parents give birth to a whirling dervish who needs constant attention, you have a problem with the fit between the parents and child. And this happens a lot. The parents may love their child, but if the first one is a whirling dervish then they may never dare to have another. They may sufficiently manage until the baby becomes a really demanding toddler. With extended families, there's often a family member who's a better match.

Polly: How do you think Barbies have affected society?

Diane: Enormously. In the world of Barbies, no one takes care of them. They have impossible bodies, impossible dimensions. Similar to Britney Spears and all the wannabe Britneys. It's had an effect on girls—no matter how many times you tell them Barbie's body is impossible to have, they don't believe you, because there it is in front of them, Barbie in their hands, Britney on the TV screen. It becomes, "She's so pretty and so popular. She has beautiful clothes. She has a boyfriend." Barbie doesn't have any parents; it's very interesting. She has a sister, but no parents. She has a house, swimming pool, Jeep, but she never has any parents or adults around. She's not portrayed as a down-and-out orphan. She's ideal. I think it's been very confusing for girls.

Diane explained that if a child gets fundamentals in the family at important stages of development, he or she won't be overwhelmed easily by the shock of puberty or by anything else.

Polly: How do we put the unhealthy family back together?

Diane: The good-enough mother or good-enough father can step in when things are heading a little bit off track. Development never goes in a straight line. We have to keep guiding it.

Polly: How does that work when there's a single mom who works—or worse, is doing drugs?

Diane: Extremely poorly. The child needs consistency and a loving person who is accessible. In a family with good-enough loving, there can be normal reworking of earlier issues.

Susan: Sands played Russian roulette at her mother's head when her mother was asleep. Something awful had to have been happening at a very early age. The divorce...

Diane: The divorce, plus fighting and divided loyalty for the child. The parents probably put the child in an impossible position well before the divorce. And the child who is trying to cope, learns to "divide and conquer." Every child tries this to some extent, and when it doesn't work he tries more subtle ways of achieving goals. For the child who can divide and conquer—with the parents in the same home or after the divorce—that's a terrible way for him to approach problem solving. Children who have been hurt can live with a lot of problems in their family if they're given love. They may grow up to have enormous inner struggles, but at least they're somewhat prepared to deal with them. A lot of these children you have visited and worked with haven't been given the basics.

In the animal kingdom, a lot of creatures get up and walk shortly after birth. Built in, inborn in some way, and crucial for survival. Most young animals who stay deep within the herd don't get eaten. In our species and in our country, in this day and age, you don't generally get eaten if you can't keep up. You grow up terribly incapable and confused and conflicted, but you do generally grow up and continue to live.

Susan: So the key is to modulate through controlling stages, to build confidence—with a sense of well-being and boundaries—in a safe environment.

Diane: In a safe enough environment, good enough. Some kids describe their parents being on drugs, but the grandmother was always there—one special person in the house. Maybe she just sat in her chair and she was blind, but she was there.

"One special person." One person who is "good enough." Such a person, consistently present in a child's life, can essentially save him or her from the consequences of bad parenting, even abuse and neglect by overwhelmed, immature, or ignorant parents.

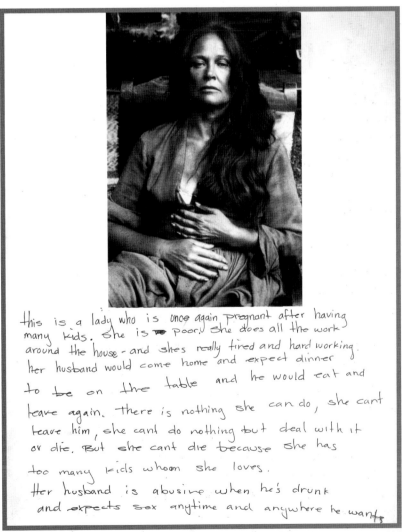

this is a lady who is once again pregnant after having many kids. She is to poor, she does all the work around the house - and shes really tired and hard working. her husband would come home and expect dinner to be on the table and he would eat and leave again. there is nothing she can do, she cant leave him, she cant do nothing but deal with it or die. But she cant die because she has too many kids whom she loves. Her husband is abusive when he's drunk and expects sex anytime and anywhere he wants

Colleen Dewhurst in *The Cowboys* – Photo by Bob Willoughby   Chim (girl), age 16

it is The wellldnes The

som of my homBoys had tag uP the Some of the walls Because hade Nthing to do so thay did Not get cot because the Pigs are stopid and thay suck.

Ongoing Trauma
Neurobiological Impacts

*These derailments of development early on lead to lifelong
incapacities that are then passed on to the next generation.*

—**Diane Campbell,** M.D.

In his eye-opening article "Traumatized Children: How Childhood Trauma Influences Brain Development,"
Dr. Bruce Perry summarizes the effects of trauma, abuse, and neglect on the developing child.

Traumatized Children

...In the United States alone from 1996 to 1998 there were more than five million
children exposed to some form of severe traumatic event such as physical abuse,
domestic and community violence, motor vehicle accidents, chronic painful medical procedures, and natural disasters... Beginning with Lenore Terr's landmark
work, investigators over the last twenty years have determined that more than
30 percent of children exposed to these kinds of traumatic events will develop serious and chronic neuropsychiatric problems...

Trauma and the Developing Brain

To help [millions of] traumatized children, we need to understand how the brain
responds to threat, how it stores traumatic memories and how it is altered by
the traumatic experience... [The] brain is designed to change in response to pat-
terned, repetitive stimulation. And the stimulation associated with fear and trauma changes the brain...

By shaping the developing brain, experiences of childhood define the adult.
Neurodevelopment is characterized by (1) sequential development and "sensitivity" (the brain "grows" from brainstem to the cortex) and (2) "use-dependent" organization ("use it or lose it")... Simply stated, children reflect the world in which
they are raised. If that world is characterized by threat, chaos, unpredictability,
fear, and trauma, the brain will reflect that by altering the development of the
neural systems involved in the stress and fear response.

The Neurobiological Responses to Threat

When a child is threatened, various neurophysiological and neuroendocrine responses are initiated. If they persist, there will be "use-dependent" alterations in the key neural systems involved in the stress response...

Another set of neural systems that becomes sensitized by repetitive stressful experiences are the catecholamine systems... These key neuro-chemical systems become altered following traumatic stress. The result is a cascade of associated changes in attention, impulse control, sleep, fine motor control, and other functions mediated by the catecholamines. As these catecholamines and their target regions (e.g., amygdaloid nuclei) also mediate a variety of other emotional, cognitive, and motor functions, sensitization of these systems by repetitive re-experiencing of the trauma leads to dysregulation in many functions. A traumatized child may, therefore, exhibit motor hyperactivity, anxiety, behavioral impulsivity, sleep problems, tachycardia, and hypertension...

—Bruce Perry, M.D., Ph.D

The earlier we can intervene, Perry concludes, the more likely that the child will be able to preserve his potential and express it.

Polly and I next spoke with Dr. Diane Campbell about the impact of trauma resulting from emotional abandonment.

The brain has a bottom-up organization. The bottom regions (i.e., brainstem and midbrain) control the most simple functions such as respiration, heart rate, and blood pressure regulation, while the top areas (i.e., limbic and cortex) control more complex functions such as thinking and regulating emotions.

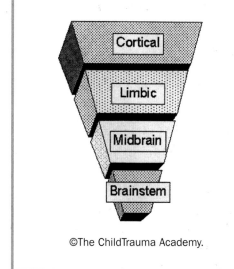

©The ChildTrauma Academy.

Diane: The worst trauma occurs when there's no supportive person in the child's life. As we discussed, this is especially true when the protector is the abuser. These children are truly emotionally abandoned.

Susan: What behavior do you see with an emotionally abandoned child?

Diane: A huge range, from total apathy and withdrawal all the way through to violence, sexual acting out, drug abuse—the really major problems. When adolescence comes along it's terribly disruptive from within. Children haven't gained that sense of basic safety. There's no safe childhood to look back to. Teenagers need to negotiate their life, living with one foot grounded in childhood and one foot looking forward with the anticipation of adulthood. But here we're talking about kids who have no safe childhood to stand on, and their sense of adulthood is a place of violence. Those kids are desperate for stimulation and a gang will substitute for family. There's no safe anchor.

Susan: The juveniles in the Hall said and wrote some insightful and brilliant things, yet demonstrated immaturity at the same time, preventing them from keeping up with their age group.

Diane: With arrested development and lack of skills to deal with adolescence, young people can't progress into adulthood. The gap between them and their peers continues to widen.

Donaldson (boy), age 17

The well-adjusted kids are progressing toward adulthood. The teenagers who cannot progress through a healthy adolescence get into drugs, violence, and promiscuity. They gang together. No one else to go to and they don't have a family. Human beings are pack animals. Very few of us do well totally alone.

Susan: So when trauma has taken place, and things haven't been mended, the cycle goes on.

Diane: Yes. Early-intervention programs try to help very early on. But these kids continue to live in abusive situations where the primary bonds are dreadful.

Susan: I sense primitive relationships. The empty, hurting teenager may remember the smell of her mother, even the taste of the food she prepared. They fantasize with raw emotions over those early memories. They even call it love.

Diane: Yes, and it's only a fantasy. Very regressive at this age. Nothing is built on top to connect them to where they need to be. The good feeling associated with the smell of your mother won't help much when you go out into the world. You need so much more—structure, a sense of separateness, autonomy, creativity. The reassuring smell of mother—or the smell of Linus's blanket, which is just one step beyond that—won't help you to be you, won't help you function in this world.

We already talked about transitional objects, but it's worth revisiting, especially as it ties into object permanence. David Winnicott called the transitional object the first "not me"

Do you feel your contribution can help kids stay out of trouble? If not, what needs to happen? NO, I NEED MONEY

I am a young person scared about the future. I am scared that I might die

I am a young adult, but I can graduate from high school and I am worried about:
a) AIDS
b) KIDS (more)
c) FAMILY

I want money & sex.

I hope that I get it.

I feel like crying.

I yell **when I am upset.**

I wish I could be alone and find some peace and quiet. If I could then everything would be all right. Then I would think.

I have 4 **brothers and sisters.**

I wish at times someone would understand me. That person would be my mentor **to me.**

I feel education is important.

If I could share something special with you I would tell you I NEED HELP.

possession. It's not a thumb, which is part of you. It's not Mommy, either. It's a possession—a teddy bear, a blanket.

Around the age of one, when the baby begins to walk and becomes involved in the outside world, the transitional object is periodically set aside. The child has to go looking for it; unlike the thumb, it's not always there. Sometimes the child panics when he can't find the object—"Where's my blanky? Find my blanky, it's gone!" When he finds it again, he begins to understand object permanence; it's the same object—the same blanky—when it comes back. It's similar to peek-a-boo—which then becomes hide-and-seek, which turns into infinite variations of the theme all the way through life. If you hide behind something and then pop back out, it's wonderfully exciting for little kids. It's a great discovery, like gravity—that's why a baby will drop something from the highchair 50,000 times. The family interacts, loving the baby's huge delight and somehow dealing with their frustration of constantly having to continue to pick up the toy on the ground.

> No baby will play peek-a-boo halfway through his first year if he's apathetic or failing to thrive. If he can't play peek-a-boo, things probably are not going well.
>
> —Diane Campbell, M.D.

No baby will play peek-a-boo halfway through his first year if he's apathetic or failing to thrive. If he can't play peek-a-boo, things probably are not going well. How do you build upon a sense of object permanence if you haven't developed it as a baby?

There's something besides physical object permanence. There's the sense of object constancy. Mommy is the same mommy no matter what her mood is. She has many facets to her, but she's still the same mommy. She's still loving even when she gets mad for a little while, and she's still there! This is how children think when physical object permanence goes well. In the Hall, we're talking about a lot of human beings where it hasn't gone well.

Susan: Where girls and even the boys focus on having their own babies.

Polly: Some of the girls in the Hall think that being pregnant and having babies is their job.

Diane: Right. You have sex, and everything else follows.

Susan: They aren't very interested in school. They say that they want an education, but they don't go for it. What did their writings tell you?

Diane: From the sampling, the level of cognitive ability varied widely as well as some of their fine motor skills. Children who don't write clearly are ridiculed and not helped with it in the third grade and beyond. For most kids, it's quite an accomplishment, between third and fourth grade, to move into cursive. Making that change is so hard when kids haven't perfected the first step.

Susan: Many children don't know what family life is like.

It was at this time that I shared with Diane an interview an inmate had created while she was incarcerated at VSP (Valley State Prison in Chowchilla, California). I had interviewed her when she was housed in the local jail, awaiting her trial for attempting to kidnap one of her two children from foster care. The girl was 18 at the time and pregnant with her third child. She experienced the grief and pain of losing all three children to the child welfare portion of probation as her prison term was lengthy and she had no family to care for the babies.

Diane: Think of the kids who don't know what it's like to experience family. This inmate wrote to you from prison and shared her fascinating response to "What's your idea of family?" The response was, *"A family is something you read about in a fairytale."* It was beautiful. That's this powerful longing and sadness. The same person said being in prison kept her off of drugs. Then in response to "When you get out of prison will you go back to drugs?" "Oh yeah!" These people feel so awful inside themselves. She avoided foster homes by lying about her age therefore being sent to jail instead of Juvenile Hall. Next, she challenges you with her attitude of, "Are you going to abandon me like the foster homes?" Trying to pull you into the struggle of either the two-year-old stage or the adolescent stage—a control struggle. It's a classic line—"You don't know what it's like to go to jail." And she doesn't know what it's like to have a family. It's scary—a young adult with no tools to rely on.

Susan: She had the three babies at ages 16, 17, and 18. She lived with friends who had babies, too. She also lived on the streets and went to a teen center for milk and diaper handouts. The babies were more like attempts to have something to love.

Diane: And there lies another issue. When the mom has a baby for her own comfort reasons. The baby begins to separate, naturally, and will crawl away, expecting Mom to go after him and pick him up. This is so much fun! But if Mom is mad she might pick that baby up in an awful way, losing a crucial opportunity. So many things come into play for the healthy mom to deal with, let alone for someone repeatedly incarcerated and lacking formal education and family ties.

Polly: So a child's independence sends an unhealthy mom into anger?

Diane: Actually, a depression. Fury. Often this echoes back to her own early beginning issues. Many will get pregnant again when the baby becomes independent. "Do I want another baby who's just going to leave me? But I want a baby to hold, I'll figure the rest out later."

Baby to infuriating toddler—figuring the rest out later is harder than it looks. When the first signs of toddlerhood begin at around 18 months, most mothers say, "I wish I had my baby back again, I wish I had my cuddly baby." These are normal feelings and how any mother deals with those depends on her own inner psychological structure. The mother in severe inner distress is not prepared psychologically for the demands of parenting a toddler.

Our reading of Perry and our conversations with Diane made a number of things clear about ongoing trauma. First, the longer the traumatizing circumstance—including emotional abandonment—lasts, the more severe the effects will be upon brain and endrocine function and therefore on behavior, especially impulse control. And when traumatized boys and girls begin having children before maturing and coming to terms with their own trauma, they repeat the destructive cycle; stressed out mothers and fathers traumatize their own children because they don't know any other way to behave. And sometimes they have more babies simply because it's too painful for an immature mother to see her cuddly infant become a stubborn and demanding toddler.

Homeless Affraide
Lost in the world

Joseph Minton, age 16

Killing Punks

Hitting the Pipe

On top of the world

Having Sex

Bramble (boy), age 17

10

The Boys' Units
Sex, Drugs, Confusion

A judge would say, "Well, what do you want to happen to you?" and this youth who you've been talking to and who's been crying and telling you all this stuff won't say a thing. There's a soft little child inside. That's why they need more advocates to speak for them...
Most of them join gangs because they need a family, protection, to feel important.
At 11 or 12, they're scared of facing the world alone.

—**Beth Shoesmith**, former Public Defender

It was now time to move into the boys' units and get a feel for their side of confinement. We already knew that there were many more boys than girls in the Hall. Thus more organization was required for handling and managing so many youths per unit. The boys did not have the freedom to meet with us in small groups as the girls did.

Polly and I met once again with the director of the facility to discuss the boys' side of the Hall, their behavior, and what we should expect when we arrived in their units. Sara reviewed with us what clothing we should wear and what supplies we could use during our visits. No pens, no music or coloring tools. We would be working with larger groups of kids at one time than on the girls' side, as each of the boys' units house up to 60 youths. Overall, the Hall housed around 90 percent boys and 10 percent girls.

> **Sara**: The Hall has the most negative kids in San Diego. Occasionally, good kids land here through no fault of their own, but very rarely. As a group, these kids are anti-authoritarian. They simply are; it's the code of the street, and it's very difficult to deal with.
>
> There was an 11-year-old boy in the 1200 Unit who was charged with possessing a rifle. He ended up on suicide watch and was moved out quickly to a more therapeutic environment. Unfortunately, we have other kids who are perhaps just as disturbed but don't get treatment.
>
> One of the things you can never measure is prevention. Sometimes a youth ends up here because he's violated probation, or not going to school, or has possessed a gun. We may have prevented a terrible crime from happening, but we'll never know for sure.
>
> We have boys' units designated for specific groups of kids. All the really young kids—the "ankle biters"—are in one unit, tiny junior-high-school kids who spend half their time wanting to play with teddy bears and the other half preening like little roosters. We put our "newborns"—the ones who come in for the first time—in another unit, very structured. We keep the 14-to-17-year-old first-timers out of the sophisticated arena. We have a separate unit for Spanish speakers. A separate unit for clients accused of assassinations or attempted murder—maximum security.
>
> We have a lot of young men who act out with sexual gestures; at any given time we have 30

to 40 sex offenders here. They drop their drawers, they masturbate, they do a lot of flashing.

Any reaction like laughing and they know that they've got you.

We spent three hours in two of the boys' units that night. As we entered the older boys' unit—1400 Unit—showers were just finishing. The coach at the control desk inside the unit watched each boy as he moved past the privacy half-screen in front of the bank of showers.

Each boy, wearing a towel wrapped around his waist, turned away from the screen to return to his cell. Many looked our way, some with attitude. A few avoided our eyes, probably shy with modesty. Within minutes they were all front and center, dressed, seated neatly at 10-foot-long tables, and ready for business.

> **DoN't forget me**
> **PleaSe**
>
> Questionnaire
> boys night 1
>
> **Packet Number:** 6
>
> Initials: ___
> Unit: 1200
> Age: 17
>
> **1) Is this your first time being in Juvenile Hall? If not, how many times have you been there?** Iue been here one time ANd its my last time.
>
> **a) Is Juvenile Hall like you thought it would be? Why/why not?** Yes a place I don't want to be because I miss my family ANd girl
>
> **b) When you get out of Juvenile Hall what would you like to accomplish for other young people so they don't have to experience Juvenile Hall?** god I would tell then to always listen to their mom + Pad I didN't.

Bramble (boy), age 17

We had created photo sheets showing a range of images, with white space below for writing. We handed them out and asked the boys to write something about what the image meant to them. The photos interested all of them. A couple of boys were concerned that they couldn't write well, but took a pencil and scratched away. After this assignment, we asked them to answer a few questions on the questionnaire Polly and I designed for them. This exercise required concentration. The unit grew remarkably quiet. I was impressed how seriously they took to the work. I picked up one of the boy's questionnaires and he pointed to something he had written—"Don't forget me please."

Compared to our encounters in the girls' units, this experience was more structured and intense. In both of the boys' units that night we witnessed many reactions, attitudes, and forms of behavior. Some of these youths had little grasp of the impact of what they'd done. Nor were they necessarily learning anything from being locked up, since no coach could provide what they'd missed by not growing up in a healthy family. Several appeared at ease as they filled out the questionnaires, while expressing anger at the outside world in what they wrote, leaving us wondering if what they missed on the outside was control.

Polly and I talked about these kids on the way home that night. It was scary to think about how some of these kids would react when they left the Hall: with clear rules and a solid structure supporting them, some might assume a new power from having been incarcerated. That power would not be consistent with behavioral change or further educational progress. They might move further from the kind of experiences necessary for them to have healthy relationships and lead productive lives.

Before we began to visit Juvenile Hall, we had met with attorney Beth Shoesmith, a public defender who worked directly with kids in the justice system. The more time we spent in the Hall, the more her insights made sense to us.

1) Is this your first time being in Juvenile Hall? If not, how many times have you been there? *I five time*

   a) Is Juvenile Hall like you thought it would be? Why/why not? *No because poeple say it fun but it not.*

   b) When you get out of Juvenile Hall what would you like to accomplish for other young people so they don't have to experience Juvenile Hall? *Tell them to stay out.*

2) Do you think after you're released you'll come back? If not, what will you do to make sure you won't return? *Stay off drug.*

3) Are you in school? If not do you have any plans to go back and finish? *Yes I have plans I want finish school because I want a good job.*

4) Do you have a positive role model that you can talk to? *N/A*

5) Do you have any family members that have been, or are in jail or prison? *my Brother* ~~████~~

6) What are your plans for the future? *Do good have a job*

7) What have you given deep thought to since you have been in Juvenile Hall? *N/A*

8) If you have one wish to change something in your life, what would it be? *To never do no drug.*

Chen (boy), age 16

Beth: A lot of dependency kids come to the court for abuse and neglect, and many graduate into the delinquency system. The government doesn't do a very good job of replacing people's parents, and kids' needs are not met, or they've been damaged. When they become teenagers, they start to act out and become delinquents.

A very large percentage of these kids are learning disabled or have various neurological or emotional problems. The school system doesn't have the money to deal appropriately with them, so they get shoved into the delinquency system. Take a child identified with a neurological condition. Teachers have tried to work with him over the years. In junior high, he pushes a teacher, or has a knife in his backpack. He's now a felon, and goes into the correctional system, which isn't prepared to deal with his problems, and doesn't do anything for them. The kids who are mentally ill, or have learning disabilities, or can't read—the educational system doesn't work at all. It takes a parent who is very knowledgeable, very determined, and very aggressive to get a child the help he needs through the public school system. He needs special tutoring, special education, counseling, psychotherapy, and possibly medication.

Susan: Are kids who use street drugs predisposed to mental illness?

Questionnaire: RC
boys night 1

Packet Number:

Initials:
Unit: 900
Age: 15

1) Is this your first time being in Juvenile Hall? If not, how many times have you been there? NO "7" praying to God to put me ON the path to positive. And stay out of trouble.

a) Is Juvenile Hall like you thought it would be? Why/why not? YAH, NO privalleges. No freedom.

b) When you get out of Juvenile Hall what would you like to accomplish for other young people so they don't have to experience Juvenile Hall? These Tell them that crime doesnt pay. But hay no ones perfect. We all make mistakes.

2) Do you think after your release, you'll come back if not, what will you do to make sure you won't return? Hopefully Not because I really want to be with my family. Get back in school, And change this negative stuff to positive.

3) Are you in school? If not do you have any plans to go back and finish? Yes, I really want to get out of here, and get some credits, This place is punishment. School yes.

4) Do you have a positive role model that you can talk to? Not really but I really would want one to be there for me.

5) Do you have any family members that have been, or are in jail or prison? NO

6) What are your plans for the future? To become a doctor or football player or work for the county.

7) What have you given deep thought to since you have been in Juvenile Hall? That I need to really straighten up and do good. I know I can. My Parents tell me I can.

8) If you have one wish to change something in your life, what would it be? To start my life all over. Not to die or anything.

9) Remember when you used to dream as a small child. What did you want to be when you grew up? A doctor!!

10) Have you ever been subjected to peer pressure? If so, how did it make you feel? How would you change it if you could and why? Yes, your a wimp you cant do it. Don't listen to them. Listen to parents.

11) What was your most memorable event (in your past)? when I turned 10 and got a Nintendo and started to be someone.

12) Do you feel your contribution can help kids stay out of trouble? If not, what Yes, All I have to do is tell them my past and guide them. Tell them to make positive descissions!!

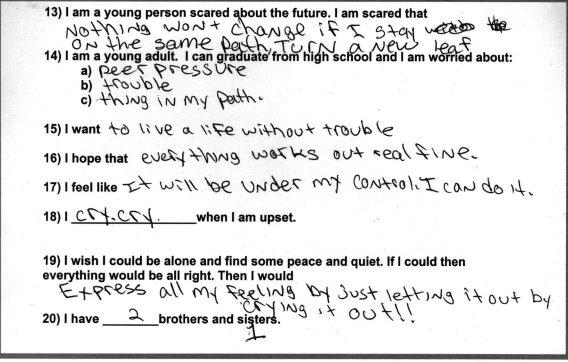

13) I am a young person scared about the future. I am scared that
Nothing won't change if I stay ~~weee the~~
on the same path, Turn a New leaf

14) I am a young adult. I can graduate from high school and I am worried about:
   a) peer pressure
   b) trouble
   c) thing in my path.

15) I want to live a life without trouble

16) I hope that everything works out real fine.

17) I feel like It will be under my control. I can do it.

18) I cry.cry. when I am upset.

19) I wish I could be alone and find some peace and quiet. If I could then everything would be all right. Then I would
Express all my feeling by Just letting it out by crying it out!!

20) I have 2 brothers and sisters.
1

Brown (boy), age 15

Beth: No, no, although it's often exacerbated by drugs. A lot of psychologists think some kids use street drugs as an attempt to self-medicate. For example, cocaine gives ADD kids the same thing some of the prescribed medications do—it helps them focus and think clearly. And kids suffering from serious clinical depression might take one of the euphoria-inducing drugs. To say the child is breaking the law by taking illegal drugs is a pretty superficial analysis of what's really going on, and what needs to be done for that child.

We had one youth in Juvenile Hall who was chewing his arm raw. Probation referred him to County Mental Health. They sent him back, saying he was manipulative. The court sent him again to County Mental Health, which again refused treatment. The judge placed him in a private psychiatric hospital, where the next day he tried to kill himself, and then ran away from the facility. He's been rearrested and put into the dependency system. We try to get these kind of kids into the dependency system, to get social services. The problem is, social services has a limited budget and they don't want kids who are over about 12.

Susan: So the 14-year-old who's been through the system a few times, what happens to him?

Beth: Oh, boy. With a troubled history, he'll come in and we'll try to divert him. Probation doesn't really go out and make contact with these kids, or follow up. Many of our lawyers will follow up and keep tabs on them, but what they need is support—family or community support, a minister, a teacher who cares.

Susan: How many kids do we have in the 12-to-18 age group?

Beth: There are 6,000 delinquents.

Susan: Solutions?

Beth: We need mentoring programs and treatment programs to turn some of these kids around. The community support needs to be out there, the dependency system needs to be willing to take kids who are properly dependents, the mental-health system needs to provide care and treatment and follow-up for kids who have mental health concerns, the school system needs money to place and treat kids who have learning disabilities. I mean, what do they think the kid is going to do who gets to be 16 years old and can't read?

Most of the kids are terrified when they go to court. They can barely speak. One common problem for our lawyers is that the children are not able to articulate their positions very well. A judge would say, "Well, what do you want to happen to you?" and this youth who you've been talking to and who's been crying and telling you all this stuff won't say a thing. There's a soft little child inside. That's why they need more advocates to speak for them. It's shocking to people to see skimpy arms and legs in court. The kids may be tough and street-wise in certain ways, but when they're out of that element, they're really lost. Most of them join gangs because they need a family, protection, to feel important. At 11 or 12, they're scared of facing the world alone.

I am a young person scared about the future. I am scared that
I might get 25-L or Die in the ~~shot~~ ghtto

I want help to get out the ghtto

I hope that one day I can Look Back ana say I Learn some thing from all this

I feel like theny no hope for us ghtto kid's

I _get High_ **when I am upset.**

I have _11_ **brothers and sisters.**

Jones (boy), age 16

And then you think about all the money that could have been saved by teaching him how to read. And those kids at a younger age could be helped, but by the time they're teenagers, it's difficult. It's not impossible. We have a former client who admitted to two attempted murders, had been in the youth authority for years, and called up and said, "I'm doing well, I've got a job, I've got a family, I've turned my life around, and I really have you to thank." I don't believe that people are really beyond saving. A lot of kids respond well to someone they think cares about them because no one really has.

Susan: The bad 28-year-old criminal is one thing, but a 14-year-old, it's perplexing.

Beth: The question is, what are we going to do about it? We've deteriorated to this point. I can't see how a wholesale move toward locking them up is going to help. You can't keep them all there forever.

I see the positive stories, then I see all the kids who are not given that opportunity, and my heart breaks for them. Nobody knows what's going to work with a particular kid, and nobody knows at what point a particular person is ready to face his or her problems. Drug ad-

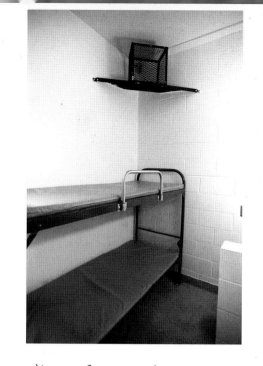

To me This is a
cell in C.Y.A
were they put kind
that do shite Bad
enough Bad thing
and they have a lote
of Time to do
This is a cell
That I might
Be in one day
if I keep going
the way I am going
People die in they's
Place every day
it is no place
to Be You come
out of your cell
for one houre a day

You fell all alone in
this place you some
Time's finay Your self
crying You some time's
fell that You will Nevery
get out You fell pain
You tell Your self
did I get here
I'm I Real here or
is it a dream They
will give You a day
when You can go home
But how to say that
You will Live that Long
in a place Like this
were every one out to get thery
and they Dont give fuck about You
or what You are going throu
so to sum it all up it
is Liveing hell But the call it C.Y.A

1) What was a typical summer for you as a child?

geting high stiling a car's geting it to truBle with my home Boy see some on die that all.

2) What are you going to be doing this summer?

I'm going to ~~Be~~ Be lock up

3) What would you like to be doing this summer?

Seeing my kid's PLay with him and her kick Back with thery mom ana my home Boy's

4) What would you like to be doing next summer?

working geting off Proroull tell my home boy's to slowe thery Rodl Be for it is to Leat

dicts and alcoholics have to hit bottom and ask for help; it's the same with these kids, but we need to be there for them and provide the environment to help them change. If they haven't been able to trust people up to the age of 15...

Susan: Are kids suspicious of people who come in and offer help?

> Most of our clients are boys, 16, 17 years old, and a lot of them already have a baby of their own.
>
> —**Beth Shoesmith**, *former Public Defender*

Beth: Most of them have a protective shell around them, but they respond well to anyone who's honest with them and acts like they really care. Some people have a talent for working with children and some don't. We have talented people in our office who get kids to tell them the most amazing things. I think a lot of people out there would like to do this work. It's just the question of having the resources. I could use another 10 social workers in my office talking to these kids. I could use another 10 people following up with these kids.

Probation departments are supposed to follow the kids, make contact with them, check their schools for attendance, check with families, create positive connections, keep them out of trouble until they're old enough to think rationally, get them involved with sports so they don't have time to get into trouble. But we're dealing with poverty-stricken people, large numbers of kids with parents on drugs, parents who don't even show up.

Susan: But how do you import love, affection, caring?

Beth: After-school programs hook some of these kids in, community programs—to be in a safe place rather than on the street where they might be shot. Our parks are pretty much taken over by gangs. Kids need a safety net. If we don't do something about this, we'll all pay the price. They'll be breaking into my house, your car, or worse.

Susan: Any advice on how Polly and I can learn more?

Beth: Sit in juvenile court and watch the proceedings. Different kinds of kids enter. See what they look like, what the judges say. Get permission from the presiding judge to sit in his courtroom. Kids in custody are brought in, advised of the charges within 48 hours. You'll hear an argument over where they'll be released—to the home, to a relative, or to custody in Juvenile Hall until the case can be heard. You'll hear the lawyer for the child give his version of what's going on, why he's not a risk, why he should go home, why the court should release him to the parents' custody until the case comes up.

Most of our clients are boys, 16, 17 years old, and a lot of them already have a baby of their own. Their hopes for their children are just the same as anybody's; they want to get straight and raise their kids right. But the baby is with the mom, who's living with her parents. This guy will go away for a period of time, return, and the baby's mom has a new boyfriend. That's the end of that relationship, and often a new cycle of unhealthy parenting starts with the baby.

When a youth is arrested, if his parents are educated and talk nicely to law enforcement and probation officers, if they show up, if they have private health insurance and can enroll their child in the McDonald Center for drug treatment, he might do OK. The parents have resources. Another kid arrested for the same thing, whose parents are dysfunctional and don't even show up for the probation interview—he gets treated harshly, even though he deserves help as much as the other kid.

Courtroom Trial

Judge: Somebody had better start speaking.

Public Defender: All right—the minor walked away from the STOP program [a 21-day treatment commitment] and the recommendation was CYA. Dr. Vale's report says he needs 24-hour school. He's not a criminally sophisticated kid. Still, this protects society. He hasn't had the benefit of a program because he walked away from STOP, but he's been fine in Juvenile Hall.

District Attorney: I agree, but I contest the initial finding of CYA. He heard voices! I'm concerned with probation's recommendation of CYA. He has prior history. He's almost 18.

Judge: No, he's 15, he's just big. I have an educational concern for the minor. The psych issue is not resolved and remains outstanding. The offending violation was the fact that he walked away from STOP. A number of educational concerns and issues need to be addressed, even though only 70 days remain. The court will follow the recommendation of probation. The minor will continue as a ward of the court and be placed in a suitable licensed facility. Prior to completion, he should be brought back to court, as his mother has an up-and-down history.

Bramble (boy), age 17

Sex is the metaphor for intimacy,
which is the metaphor for love, which is absent.

—Vincent Felitti, M.D.

11

Sexualized Aggression
Separating Sex and Violence

If they're exploited, shamed, over-encouraged, over-stimulated, then they are confused.
Sexuality is all through us. We are all sexual creatures. We are all aggressive creatures, too...
With a lot of the sexual predators in our culture, sexuality and aggression have remained
fused. Sadism, the pleasure of inflicting pain on someone, is very scary stuff; development has
gone terribly awry, and by adolescence those kids are in deep trouble.

—**Diane Campbell**, M.D.

By now, we had met with over 100 youths in the Hall. We knew that most of these youths, children actually,
had already lost out on having a "good enough" person in their lives. Given that context, what could still
be done to change their behavior?

Diane returned to my office and we continued the conversation.

Susan: Many youths in the Hall seemed to dwell on their mothers.

Diane: They expect rejection. This is what they know. A lot of these kids have become confused in the development of their sexual and aggressive drive.

These children are often extremely shamed. Or they are over-stimulated. Or those two experiences are combined. Young children's exploration of their own bodies and to some extent the bodies of their peers, is often normal and the adults need to instill an appropriate sense of limits. If the children are exploited, shamed, over-encouraged, over-stimulated then they are confused. Sexuality is all through us. We are all sexual creatures. We are all aggressive creatures, too. And for sex to blend in an integrated way is very important and complicated. With a lot of the sexual predators in our culture, sexuality and aggression have remained fused. Sadism, the pleasure of inflicting pain on someone, is very scary stuff; development has gone terribly awry, and by adolescence these kids are in deep trouble.

Rather than working through the early stages of childhood again in adolescence, they're in such deep trouble they end up in a bizarre little containment area of society. Sexual integration isn't there. Two basic drives are very confused when kids are in this kind of trouble.

Diane's comments again brought to mind John Gardner, who is serving two consecutive life terms after confessing to raping and murdering two teenage girls. He had been freed from prison several years before, despite a previous conviction that forced him to register as a sex offender. He had also had several run-ins with law enforcement after he was released. I wondered whether earlier intervention, treatment, and supervision might have unlocked the link between sadistic violence and sex in Gardner. Could earlier intervention and more consistent supervision have prevented the deaths of Chelsea King and Amber Dubois?

Diane, Polly, and I resumed our conversation.

Susan: Predators are good at what they do. Are these people who are sometimes stuck in rage?

Diane: Sure. Especially if in truth they haven't been able to leave behind the two-year-old stage and those issues get very much kicked up in adolescence of course. Some people stay enraged in it. They can't gain insight. They can't reflect. This stuff gets going and it rocks on through life. It's those things that lead teens into the Hall.

One of the scariest things on earth is the fusion of sexuality and aggression. The fusion of experiencing pleasure and inflicting pain is very complicated developmentally, and filled with uncertainty, innuendo, and shadow.

Susan: When the protector becomes the abuser, does that have something to do with this pain/pleasure area?

Diane: The ultimate in confusion and shame is when the abuser is the protector.

Do you have any family members that have been, or are in jail or prison?
my dads doing a life sentance

What was your most memorable event (in your past)?
the very first time I robbed some one

I am a young person scared about the future. I am scared that
I wont make nothing about my life

I _get in fights_ when I am upset.

If I could share something important with you I would tell you
always look over your back and trust no one

Bass (boy), age 15

Susan: It seems to me that the individual may not experience the difference between pleasure and pain.

Diane: Yes, and that's true in the relationships between persons, and within an individual person's own psyche. You're both the giver and receiver of what goes on in your own psyche.

Polly: So the earliest relationships have a lot to do with how the person's psyche is structured?

Diane: For example, the development of what people call "remorse" occurs following a tantrum, when the mother stays present, and the exhausted toddler creeps back into her lap and gets loved. He says, "I'm sorry, Mommy," or kisses her. Love, with tenderness, touching Mommy's face is key to developing healthy remorse.

Let's look now at the child or teenager who says, "I hate myself." He is not experiencing remorse because remorse requires a climate of love. This is more self-hate in the absence of

I am a young person scared about the future. I am scared that

That there did ~~No~~ *will be in the world but me are no women*

I am a young adult. I can graduate from high school and I am worried about:
a) *Nothing*
b)
c)

I want ~~xxxxxxxxxx~~ *get more tatoos*

I hope that ~~xxxxxxxx~~ *I kick with the homies*

I feel like *having Sex*

I *have fights* when I am upset.

I wish I could be alone and find some peace and quiet. If I could then everything would be all right. Then I would *bust a fifi*

Circle one and explain to us why.

I (like/**dislike**) school? *It's Dumb*

I (like/**dislike**) my siblings. *there stupid*

I (**like**/dislike) family members. *I Love them*

I wish at times that I could live alone. (**T**/F)

I wish at times someone would understand me. That person would be
my ~~xx~~ lover to me.

I feel education is *Stupid* .

If I could share something important with you I would tell you
I'm not a Virgen.

Bramble (boy), age 17

self-love. There can't be any real forgiveness because he's not the lover and beloved, he is the hater and the hated.

Susan: What about children who have aggressive feelings that frighten them?

Diane: Children with big aggressive feelings that are not well contained are very frightened of the feelings. I think what hasn't happened for a lot of the youths in the Hall is the separation of their instincts for being sexual and their instincts for being aggressive. These have remained fused in a primitive way...

Furthermore, these kids have not developed the capacity to control these instincts. And let's look at controlled sexual and aggressive energy, and how those capacities influence a kids' ability to learn in school. Learning has a lot to do with aggressive energy. Reading is quite complex in the absence of well-sublimated aggressive energy. Reading aloud is almost impossible for the child who is too afraid to be assertive and take chances.

Curiosity is an important part of even the earliest bodily experiences and exploration. When you diaper a baby, one of the first things he does is to put a hand on his genitals, to explore the feelings and the area. By the time the child reaches the age of four, he's exploring far more of the world, relationships, and his imagination. By then he's beginning to set his own limits. By then, most children have learned, "No, we don't hit."

Affiliation: The Third Core Strength

Human beings are born dependent...

However inclined they are to group activities and behavior, humans must learn how to interact successfully within a group. We must learn how to communicate, listen, negotiate, compromise, and share with many diverse people in many situations. These social skills are not always easy to master...

Some children manage this process well. Others do not; these tend to be children with immature attachment or self-regulation skills. A child's acceptance into a group depends heavily on his or her capacity to regulate anxiety, impulsive behavior, and frustration. Without these prerequisite strengths, a child will have difficulty forming and regulating the relationships with others that are necessary to develop affiliation skills. Group members will likely reject a child who is impulsive or disengaged. Unfortunately, this creates a negative cycle—having fewer opportunities to socialize leads to slower social learning. These children become more isolated from their peers. They perform poorly in group interactions and avoid opportunities to be with others.

Over time, the excluded child can take this pain and turn it inward, becoming sad or self-loathing. Or the pain can be directed outward, leading to aggression or even violence. Later, without intervention, these individuals are more likely to seek out other marginalized individuals and affiliate with them. Unfortunately, the glue that holds these groups together can be self-destructive or hateful beliefs.

—Bruce Perry, M.D., Ph.D

Who is your favorite author?

Johnny Quinonez

What do you like about this author?

the murder and rape

Remember when you used to dream as a small child. What did you want to be when you grew up?

A pimp or husler

when I look at this I see a man that
has no ProlBm'sin Life he can ~~can~~
Just kick Back he dose not
have to worey about Jail or
drive BY's or see Little kids
die to me ~~ha~~ he is ~~Ba~~ up in
the Place called haven were
Every whats to go one day
But some will never

12

Negotiating Childhood
Windows of Opportunity

How did these kids get in such a mess? To begin with, think of the kids
who don't know what it's like to be in a functioning family.

—**Diane Campbell**, M.D.

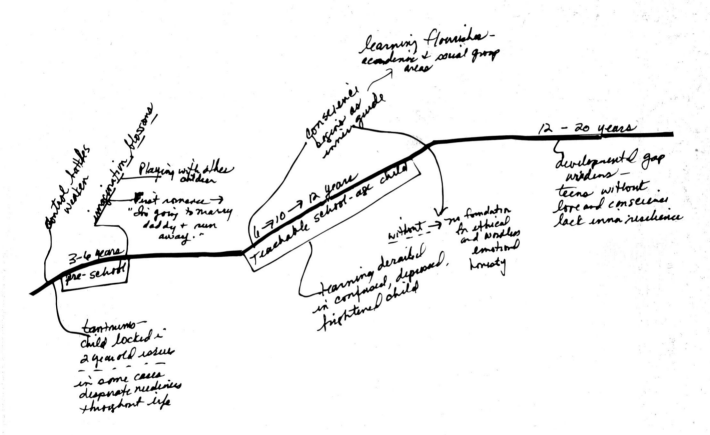

I was moved by what Diane Campbell had said. Those of us who are from relatively solid families find it hard to imagine things being any other way. It's easier to bunch these youths together into a classification—abused, damaged, or hopeless. Harsh words, yet isn't that what we, as a society, are doing essentially?

Susan: Obviously these kids are confused, acting out, and angry. How does this early confusion develop into violence?

Diane: If you negotiate the two-year-old issues well, the anger has boundaries. You become a somewhat older preschool child, and the boundaries of your anger integrate into your relationships and into your conscience. When you're really mad at age four, you might think up a story to get back at your grandmother by cooking her like the children did in "Hansel and Gretel."

By the age of six or so, when things are going pretty well, the child's conscience is beginning to be useful. And for the next several years until puberty, children with a pretty-well-functioning conscience get to practice it within their relationships and within themselves.

Think how interfering it is when the years of the teachable school-age child are cut short by an early puberty and once again, the sexual and aggressive impulses are dominant in life. Girls reach puberty earlier than boys do.

Susan: So sexual and aggressive impulses are powerful during puberty. What do we mean by the term "passive aggressive" applied to the youths in the Hall?

Diane: The passive-aggressive human being says, "Sure, I'll take out the garbage," but he deliberately doesn't do it. That's passive aggressive, no intention. Whereas if he says, "Oh my god, I forgot," and then does it, that's a functional person. It's a function of conscience.

These kids in the Hall appear to be passive aggressive, but they don't actually experience impulse and consequence, action and consequence. They're often unable to have empathy, because they're so self-preoccupied. They think in terms of "It was fun! Whee!" These kids, by the time they get in Juvenile Hall, have experienced their own aggression run amuck. Most of them do not have the developmental foundation to deal with that type of aggression. They haven't learned how to be aggressive in a humane sense—assertive, self-protective, and protective of the vulnerable around them, their own babies or the elderly. They are needy. They are emotionally distressed. Taking drugs and thieving is appealing.

Susan: Does sexual acting out escalate with the aggression?

Diane: Human sexuality and aggression begin to develop in early stages of childhood. The instincts are not well separated from each other early in life. But as children turn four, five, they do separate the instincts, and that's where they become very sexually interested and ask questions about where babies come from. Curiosity is developing. However, if you watch the lives of people who become very disordered in their personality development, they never separate out these instincts. They rape. That's an aggressive act—sexual aggression.

Susan: Going back to a little boy in Judge Pate's courtroom... The sexual activity he was accused of was profound for any age and he was only 11. He was from a disorganized house-

---

I am a young person scared about the future. I am scared that
I might die

I am a young adult, but I can graduate from high school and I am worried about:
a) AiDS
b) KiDS (more)
c) FAmily

Jackson (boy), age 17

THiS iS A DRUNK
FUCKEN DOG
MELLIESTER WHO iS
ABOUT TO CROSS
THE STREET AND
Get HiT BY A
CAR FOR BeiNG
DRUNK AND A
DUM SHit FOR
WEARING A COSTUM
NOT ON HALLOWEEN
AND iS BLIND
BECAUSE
HiS DOG HAD
SHOT SOME SPErm
iN HiS EYES
AND iS ABOUT TO
START STRiPiNG
AND DANCING
ON tHE POLE

Lonquist (boy), age 16

hold. He was living what he saw. What ages are most vulnerable? What age would be deemed as incapable of change?

Diane: I think children are very reachable and very malleable, but this is difficult work. The five- and six-year-olds are still malleable. When you get up to about age eight it gets very difficult to bring about change in the very foundations of development. You can help them out but it's difficult to change that basic stuff. There is a window of opportunity and when the window begins to close, basic change becomes really difficult. During puberty and adolescence, personality development is pretty shaken again, and there's an opportunity for reworking to occur. But it's really hard to do. It requires a lot from the teenager and a consistent adult.

Susan: How do these difficulties with sexual and aggressive development impact learning?

Diane: When girls have not had their basic needs of nurturing and bonding met, they very often fall off the learning curve around sixth grade. That's because the teaching style demands executive functioning—the ability to sequence a task, figure out how to get from here to there, divide the material and conquer. Tuning out from educational demands is common. We all do that when we're tired, angry, irritated, not feeling well—and it doesn't impact our lives in a horrible way. But for these kids, tuning out and suffering the con-

One of the things about little children is that they go through stages where they feel strong for a while and then they feel really shaken and uncertain when they transition into another stage.

—Diane Campbell, M.D.

sequences is an everyday experience. They just can't put the whole learning thing together.

One of the things about little children is that they go through stages where they feel strong for a while and then they feel really shaken and uncertain when they transition into another stage. A nine-year-old might look like she's dealing with a trauma better than the 13-year-old. The 13-year-old might have a terrible time holding it all together in the face of trauma, because all of life places her right on the edge. In early adolescence emotion spills all over. By middle adolescence kids start to get more organized.

Susan: I sense most of the youths in the Hall are going through transitional stages and already feeling disrupted. Their brains are needing more rest rather than more agitation. Do we ignore this in our society out of our own ignorance?

Diane: Don't you wonder? These are kids who are in unstable transitional times in development anyway, and the trick is to tell the difference between the kids who are going to do pretty much OK and the kids who are about to fall off the cliff.

Susan: When does compassion for the child develop into anger and hostility?

Diane: Compassion turns into anger and hostility when the child repeatedly does not respond well to your expectations. That's not rewarding to the adult. It's frustrating to be with that child.

For instance, children who have ADD or learning disabilities can't hold onto complex directions. Compassionate adults can become angry and hostile without understanding why. Adults want to see a child react lovingly to acts of compassion, but withdrawn and depressed children don't give that gratification back to the compassionate adult. The child who expects to be punished or abandoned, let's say the child who has been in multiple foster homes and now goes into an adoptive home, who says, "I'm gonna take charge of this. I'm gonna get rid of these people before they get rid of me"—that child finds himself feeling attached and he doesn't want to get profoundly attached because he figures these people are going to kick

I am a young person scared about the future. I am scared that *I won't finish high school*

I am a young adult. I can graduate from high school and I am worried about:
a) *my self*
b) *killing myself on the nuts*
c) *getting addicted too Drugs again*

I want *happiness in my life*

I hope that *I will have it someday*

I feel like *a rat in a cage with nowhere too go out down*

Oberlin (boy), age 16

him out. Everyone else has. So the adoptive parents, who are behaving compassionately, find themselves feeling angry and hostile.

It's very fair to say that most children have an incredible drive to develop and grow with the increasing neurological, muscular, cognitive competence, plus the physical underpinnings of psychological development. The drive to develop is really profound in children. Facilitate that with a good-enough relationship with somebody loving and steady, and a lot of children will move right along. Interfere with that by abusive or neglectful care—especially chronically abusive and neglectful care—and you begin to wonder how some kids thrive in spite of all that, because most kids don't. I have friends who have had tough childhoods and open their homes to all their kids' friends because they know what that did for them.

---

1) If you have no desire to go to a University what are your plans for the future.

    ⓐ out to make money
    ⓑ relationships with family and building a family of your own.
    c) do you think you'll be able to afford taxes, a family etc?

Write us about your thoughts. *if I don't graduate high school at least I will comitt suicide*

2) For those interested in higher education, do you think you could have a GED in 2 years? Would you want to go to a Junior College, a College, or a University? (College = city & University = private or state). *I think I could have a GED in 2 years because I'm smart I just need someone too help me*

3) Draw for us a threatening place.
    etc.

Hell

If I could share something important with you I would tell you *Why I'm fucked in the head*

Oberlin (boy), age 16

NEED TO FINISH

Questionnaire: RC
boys night 1

Packet Number: 37

Initials:
Unit: 1200
Age: 16

1) Is this your first time being in Juvenile Hall? If not, how many times have you been there?
5 OR 6 TIME

a) Is Juvenile Hall like you thought it would be? Why/why not?
YES, BECAUSE YOU HAVE TO ASK PROMISSION
FOR EVERY THING YOU DO. CAN'T USE THE RESTROOM WHENU
**b) When you get out of Juvenile Hall what would you like to accomplish for WAN
other young people so they don't have to experience Juvenile Hall?**
IF YOU DO DRUGS OR STELL ONE OF THIS
DAY IT WELL CAUGHT UP AND YOU'LL BE
IN HERE.

2) Do you think after you're released you'll come back? If not, what will you do to make sure you won't return?
I'M GOING TO STOP USEING
DRUGS. I'M GOING TO FINISH HIGH SCHOOL
AND GET MY DEPLOIMA.

3) Are you in school? If not do you have any plans to go back and finish?
I'VE BEEN TRYING TO FINISH BUT
DRUGS GOT IN THE WAY OF LEARNING.

4) Do you have a positive role model that you can talk to?
MY MOTHER

5) Do you have any family members that have been, or are in jail or prison?
MY DAD HAS BEEN LOCKED
UP MOST OF HIS LIFE.

6) What are your plans for the future?
TO FINISH HIGH SCHOOL

7) What have you given deep thought to since you have been in Juvenile Hall?
HOW HARD ITS GOING TO
BE TO STOP USEING DRUG

8) If you have one wish to change something in your life, what would it be?
THAT I NEVER STARTED
USEING DRUGS IN THE FRIST PLACE

9) Remember when you used to dream as a small child. What did you want to be when you grew up?
POLICE MAN

Graff (boy), age 16

MY DAD HAS BEEN LOCKED UP MOST OF HIS LIFE.

Graff (boy), age 16

21) I (like/dislike) school?
It doesn't go into my head.

22) I (like/dislike) my siblings.
I just dont like them

23) I (like/dislike) family members.
Their my family and they will never let me down.

24) I wish at times that I could live alone. (T/F)
because there will be nobody to tell me nothing.

25) I wish at times someone would understand me. That person would be
a friend to me.

26) I feel education is important, but boring for me.

Grant (boy), age 15

If all you see is hoods and hoodlums and proof of their
crimes, you might not choose to undergo the trauma of this
work, and it might be difficult to treat them as children.
But they're kids!

—Sara Vickers
Former Director, Kearny Mesa Detention Facility

Cameron (girl), age 14

13

Dinner Hour
Building Trust

I want to go back to school.
It's fun doing this work with you guys.

—**Hui** (girl), resident of GRF, Juvenile Hall

Many of our visits were during the GRF dinner hour. The girls were permitted to eat while talking and working with us. It was obvious which of the girls ate healthy amounts of vegetables in spite of the predominant carbohydrates served. Hui and Chim had been raised on lean meals of rice, chicken, fish, and vegetables. Sands and Minton were picky about what they ate, depending on their mood swings. Anderson focused on soft foods and sweets. She was overweight, yet still a beauty.

> **Susan**: What about eating disorders in the Hall—what causes those?

> **Diane**: Bulimic women will go for soft mushy food for comfort. They binge on it because it feels good in a bodily way; it goes down quick and easy and it's easy to throw up. Some of these girls may not be bulimic but they eat soft food for comfort. It lulls them.

On one of our visits, Anderson had told us, "You should see me on the outs. I don't eat like this. I don't weigh this much either."

As beneficial as it was for us to witness the behavior of youths locked up, we also took note of how the girls communicated while eating their dinner. Food soothed intense discussions and everyone got along, often sharing and exchanging food items.

> **Susan**: The chaos that goes on in different units—a little tough kid had to be removed from her cell and all of a sudden others copied her behavior. Powerful.

> **Diane**: Very complicated stuff—trying to change all of this. That's why we haven't done it. If it were simple we would have accomplished it instead of pouring money down the street. Through their writings I sensed many were acting out with the purpose of being loved or the need to be loved and they didn't understand how they could be loved.

During our next visit, Polly and I entered the GRF unit's conference room at 5:30 p.m., before the girls arrived. We laid out supplies and set up the music selection for the two hours with the girls. One by one Chim, Hui, Anderson, and finally Sands strolled in and sat down without saying hello or even a smile. "Sorry I'm late," Sands said, "but the coaches decided to get on my nerves."

Ignoring Sands, Anderson blurted out something about a girl in the Hall who was in for attempted murder because of beating up a pregnant woman. Then she changed the subject and said she wanted to eat dinner.

> Through their writings I sensed many were acting out with the purpose of being loved or the need to be loved and they didn't understand how they could be loved.
>
> —Diane Campbell, M.D.

Chim was working on a photo sheet. Others just sat. Hui announced that "Dr. Dread" was supposed to come to the Hall. She said she was not on any meds yet, but that she wanted to be able to go to school. "That's why I'm getting that tattoo taken off."

Hers was an awfully big tattoo, on her back, a gang-involvement signature. She had covered it with high-necked sweaters on prior visits.

Chim: That's just her race—her pride, not gang. Some people just want it to be known. We don't burn it on us, like cows. We tattoo it. It's because some people look at our race as wicked, weird, not a part of here. Not a part of them. So we say, "This is what I am—my pride. Nothing you say will get me down and make me do something."

Hui: I want to go back to school. It's fun doing this work with you guys.

It grew hot in the closed room and Polly opened the windows to the closed-in yard just outside the conference room.

Sands: I have a question. Why did you bring in *Reviving Ophelia*?

Hui: Because we were talking about Mary Pipher, the author.

Polly: Sands, what was your experience on the field trip to meet her?

Sands: I don't know. I listened to her. I liked her speech. Sometimes she was funny and sometimes she was boring.

Anderson was quiet. She got up and left the room to get food. Hui commented, "I hope it's not mashed potatoes and gravy."

Sometimes it appeared as though the girls had little to do but sit around and wait for food. When I shared this observation with Diane Campbell, she said, "Yes, they're often hungry on many levels, not just for physical food, so they try to feed their spirits by feeding their bodies and it doesn't work."

Anderson returned with macaroni and cheese, fish, and broccoli. She said the Tabasco smelled like vinegar.

Polly: How long have you and Hui known each other?

Chim: Forever.

Polly: You were like raised together? How old are you?

Chim: Fourteen.

Hui: We're a month apart.

Susan: Are you going to stay friends forever?

Chim: No. We're sisters forever. Until I die. I'm gonna sit in her grave if she dies first.

Hui talked about Sands's mother looking pretty and "too young to have a daughter like you."

Chim: You guys look like sisters.

Sands: She has four kids. She's not old but... She is old!

Chim: You know what I like to look at? I like to read children's stories. I like *A Light in the Attic* by Shel Silverstein.

Sands: You know what? It's going to be weird when I see you on the outs because I'm not mean on the outs, I'm not rude and I don't talk very much, but in here...

'Cambodia' / (sacrafice) Kampuchea

Cambodia. My people's land. The beautiful scenery. The beautiful animals,— but— The killing fields !!! All because of one stupid, greedy, uncaring communist, whom is also a Cambodian, Many have died. Pol Pot, the wanted man, has destroyed our beautiful land, killed thousands of people, and a wounded Cambodia. The wound will not heal for a long time !!! Pol Pot and his men all dressed in black with a red rag, has no heart! no feelings! no love! Those Bastards! None of them deserve to live! Hurting their own people. Making people suffer the the most painful deaths! Raping young girls! Killing newborns who barely just caught a glimse of this raging world! Kicking people on they're heads. disrespecting elders, torchure! Those dirty, ugly, no-hearted Busters deserve to die.!!! All of them.!!! All those stupid bitches who think that they're all that! huh! wait till I see there ugly faces! I'll regulate! When i get older, maybe about 3 more years, I will join the military. I would like to go help my people and our country. When I see one of them Khmer Rouge, I will give them the death penalty! I'll give them a taste of there own medicin I will slowly kill them, so they can feel the pain! I would cut a line through their head, faces and body, but not deep enough to kill them yet. then I will pour alcohol all ... over ... their ... Bodys!

then I would whip them to a bloody death til' there's no skin left on there body, then I'd cut up their body parts and feed them to the animals!

My dad even made fun of me when I was little.
Yeah, him and my brother were teasing me. Imagine
being called Little Bo Peep ever since kindergarten.
Now some people still call me Little Bo Peep.
I just got too much on my mind.

...These are just tattooed inside my head.

–**Hui** (girl), age 15

Susan: Thank you for preparing us. We're glad we get to see you.

Anderson: Sands is just tired of these females, just like all of us are.

Sands: The first week when I came to juvenile I was so nice and quiet. Ask Hui.

Polly: Is this your first time in, Sands?

Sands: Second. Half of the kids that have been in here are back.

A girl walked up to the door to the conference room and looked inside. Chim and Hui stared at her.

Chim: See that stupid girl? I wanna hit her so badly.

Hui: She's the one I told you that got into a fight in the yard.

Polly: Where did you come up with that talk?

Chim: I don't remember. Second nature. Age three. I learned to fight back. I learned by watching and doing.

Polly: How many brothers and sisters?

Chim: Which ones?

Anderson: Your blood brothers and sisters.

Chim: I have four blood brothers. Supposed to be five, but one died.

Susan: You learned to fight from your family?

Chim: Not from all of them. I'm the second oldest. But my mom used to fight a lot too, when she would have arguments with her victim... I moved here from Thailand. My mom's from Cambodia. My dad's from Cambodia.

Polly: How did you get here?

Chim: From the Khmer Rouge, the Red and the Blue... These are soldiers. OK? They put us as prisoners...my father was a soldier. *[She pauses then changes the subject.]* We don't have Christmas. We go to Vegas. My parents go to the hotel. Until my parents got split up and got divorced.

Anderson: I'm stressed so I'm eating. I'm tired of my roommate.

Polly: How does food differ in Cambodia?

Chim: Oh, the food is fresh. My dad was a farmer. He was a teacher. He taught Cambodian in Thailand.

Polly: What are the beliefs in Buddhism?

Chim: Same thing as in the Bible: no stealing, no adultery, no alcohol, don't harm, don't kill.

Anderson: You should hear those guys talk in Cambodian.

Chim: You'll catch us talking. I don't speak much English.

Susan: If I speed up the recorder... *[They laugh, hearing their sped-up voices.]*

Chim: That's Vietnamese, not Cambodian.

Hui: That sounds like a pig.

Anderson: You guys know what? I even gave up all my team clothes today. Packed up every-thing and the sheets off my bed.

Hui: What happened?

Anderson: They don't want me because...well, they want me to do a pre-placement again. I go for the whole weekend to be with the other foster girl because they don't think that I'm going to get along with her.

Chim: I got a question for you. I wanted to ask you this but I'm gonna to ask you now. And don't get an attitude with me because I'm not getting an attitude with you.

Anderson: No. I'm leaving...OK? I thought I was leaving. The last couple days for me have been really hard. I think because I'm leaving and it feels like everybody's trying to get to me. I'm mad. The coaches have been messin' with me. I wasn't arguing with the coach. I'm not going to bow down.

We talked about aspirations. Chim asked what aspirations were.

Chim: I'd like to go to college but I don't think I can. I have to finish high school first. School is hard for me. In here it's easy. I mean I'm working on pre-Algebra and I've been working on that for three years.

> I've had things taken from me when I was younger and now I'm doing that.
>
> —Chim (girl), age 15

Hui: They don't teach you here. You just read the book and do it yourself. Susan, I have this problem. Hunger for life. I'm going to be hungry for life. My mom doesn't visit me in here, only visits my brother. I've really been trying hard for my special visit with my brother. It seems not to work.

Susan: Can you show affection with your family, like a hug?
Hui: For some reason I have a problem with hugging and kissing.

Polly: Even your mom?
Hui: Yeah.

Susan: What about activities like taking things from people? Do you feel what goes around comes around?
Chim: I've had things taken from me when I was younger and now I'm doing that. Oh yeah. I was a small little girl. I usually got snatched left and right.
Sands: You wouldn't trust her at Kmart. I be going in the stores, put my hair up... I wear it down or extension, put a little clip in and it's cute, put in some earrings, put a necklace around my neck...rock out with a purse or the make-up in a purse...
Chim: I put my stuff in a planter...

Sands took the photo of Einstein.

Sands: Well, his daughter's ugly. I hate writing on old people. I don't like looking at wrinkles!
Susan: I hope you never have them, darling.
Sands: I wanna die at age 35.
Susan: Well, you're moving along that direction.

Birds chirped outside the window in the rec area. It was a pleasant evening. Anderson handed over her paper.

Polly and I returned a week later only to find there was another new coach and Anderson had gone to a foster placement. From one week to the next, there could be a new director, new coaches, kids sent home or to foster care, others returning. Restrictive premises and in-house rules remained the only consistent features.

Sands was in RC—Restricted Confinement. We walked into the conference room with Hui.

Hui: Life is boring. Anderson left. She was happy. She said she's going to write me but then I don't know. I just hope she's in a safe place. People have told me that sometimes foster homes aren't good. Everyone is leaving in our group. Me and Sands are roommates now, when she's not in RC.

(Albert Einstein)
He looks very tired.
He seems as if he's stressed
out because of his hair.
and all the wrinkles
he has. But I know he was
a very smart man. He was
a genius. He reminds me
of me when I'm tired
and stressed out. I hope
I dont have alot of
wrinkles when I'm as old
as him! But I think well
I want to be as smart as
him.

Sands (girl), age 16

But I have bad news. They want to put me on antidepressants. My psych says I have a depression problem because I talk about my frustrations and my past life too much. So they're putting me on meds, but I don't wanna be on them.

I don't really wanna testify. It's gonna involve my life. It's against homeboys. I have to make that decision and it's really hard. I've been trying to get a special visit with my brother and all I hear is that he's not gonna get to have the visit because he had a fight. That makes me mad because I try really hard but then all of a sudden they look at his behavior too and then they tell me that I can't see him until he does good...

It makes me really mad.

Susan: They're looking at your brothers differently.

Hui begins talking and skips randomly from topic to topic as they arise in her mind.

Hui: Yeah but then it's kinda because I got sentenced for so much time. People get charged with armed robbery and get less time than me and that's not right. They dropped three of my charges and now I only have two charges... My mom needs help. She's been evicted. My grandma, too. My mom works two different jobs so she doesn't have time for me. The psychs are trying to put me on Tegretol like Sands and keep me whacked out... I miss Anderson and how she be hogging up two meals. I'm on the verge of about hitting my PO. She keeps saying, "Yeah, I'll do it, I'll see what I can do..."

My brother is in 1400. He's in here for a long time. He's going to prison. He's charged with something really serious that he didn't do. It's just stressing me out 'cause the guy wants me to testify against my brothers and against those other homeboys and I don't want to testify... In a way I don't wanna leave out of this place. It's like I'm walking straight back to society and they're looking at me as if I'm a really bad person.

Polly: When you say "stressing," how do you feel? Sick? Angry?
Hui: Frustrated, angry, makes me feel sad. Makes me feel like I just wanna cry.

Susan: How did your outing go last week?
Hui: We went to see the author of *Reviving Ophelia*. She was great. She talked about the past. The past—they didn't have pornography and they weren't into drugs but now it's just changing. Girls are getting pregnant and it was... I think I got something good out of that. I wanna read it. Anderson hadn't left, yet. She went to the event too, but she just sat there falling asleep. I wanna continue on in school and I don't wanna go to school here. Coming to school here is like independent study but I'm going to be locked up in here for like 10 months.

She talked nonstop, freely and openly as we had never heard before... She had a private audience who cared about her.

Hui: I have problems with my anger because now I have to bottle it up. I'm just mad. I just want to be left alone. It's hard 'cause I don't know people. I'm afraid I'm going to just explode. I have problems with just throwing things around, tantrum.
Susan: You're too old for that.
Hui: I don't know but it's just getting... I don't know how I got that but then I remember when I was small, younger actually, I'm still small but younger than I am now, I was chasing my cousin around with a butcher knife. I was mad. Nine years old. They tried to put me in a mental hospital. My cousin's mom, my mom's sister—blood sister, my aunt— called the police on me and they took me to the hospital. They thought I was crazy. I wasn't crazy. They

This picture luks like Ther
having fun. This old ~~le~~ laedy
luks like she is Sambady
grand mather with her dator
I thinc she tuch tis pictur
becase thats her familey.
and I wish I was in that
picture.

Creighton (girl), age 15

were sticking some things on me. I was like, what are you guys doing to me?

Susan: Can you remember the moment when you grabbed the knife?

Hui: Kind of. I was really pissed off because my brothers were making fun of me. My cousins were making fun of me. For some reason I get really mad when people make fun of me.

Susan: For being the smallest in your family?

Hui: Yeah. My dad even made fun of me when I was little. Yeah, him and my brother were teasing me. Imagine being called Little Bo Peep ever since kindergarten. Now some people still call me Little Bo Peep. I just got too much on my mind. But these are just tattooed inside my head.

You guys are like a mom and a sister to me. It's hard. My mom doesn't visit me. My dad does but it's only one hour here and there. Then people call me short. I'm in a big jam. In a way I don't think I'm ready to face society. At least I have comfort with you guys.

I don't think this place is a good place, really. If you're gonna get rehabilitated why do they lock you down and tell you…just constantly remind you, "You're locked up for robbery," this and that, you know? You should at least know this and that. But in a way it's not really my fault. I don't take it as my fault. I went there to borrow some money from her and those guys took it wrong. I think, because of the crystal.

In a way I feel I'm done but I just have this feeling that if my mom moves into the wrong neighborhood it might just happen again. There's too many things that happened in the past. They say they're my friends but I take them as associates.

Polly stepped out to chat with Coach Julie.

Polly: Anderson's back?

Coach Julie: Yeah, she just came back in tonight for pre-placement. You asked about Sands. She threw something at staff today so she needed to get RC. She's had RC the last three days.

Polly: Hui seems quite disturbed and upset tonight.

Coach Julie: She should be. That's good.

Coach Julie shared a few disturbing details about Chim and the brothers being involved in a burglary and rape.

Coach Julie: The Asian gangs are real extortionists. Hui and Chim are big within the clan. They've got lots of stripes.

Anderson entered GRF. She was excited to see us. Hui beamed. Coach Julie came back for her and said, "Excuse me, Anderson, but you haven't had your urine test."

I walked out with Coach Julie and Anderson as the coach instructed her to give a sample of urine in the tiny cup. The coach continued to chat with us. She had been in the Hall when we interviewed Morinski over a year ago. She wanted us to grasp the serious nature of where these youths are coming from and headed.

Coach Julie: It's really sad. Morinski is back and has a lot of work to do. She's a lightweight in gangs, but it's amazing how much control these kids have. Hui is a big time gang-banger and Chim is her sister in crime. They're in together for the same crime.

In his applied research on aggression, psychologist Seymour Feshbach concluded that anger is an emotional reaction that culminates in hateful behavior. Children who are more empathic are less aggressive, and low-empathy children are more aggressive. Interestingly, participation in an empathy-training program reduced aggression in both aggressive and relatively nonaggressive children.

I wondered if empathy training was an approach that might prove effective with these young women.

The chain smoker.

This man is a straight-up chain smoker.
He's been smoking for years and years and
years. His breath smells _really_ bad. His hair smells
like nothing but niccotine. His clothes does too
He rarely showers, oh-maybe once or twice
a week. His jeans are probably torn up and old.
He probably has kids but is not married. He's in
his late 30's, he lives in a small little studio with
his pal. He's a trashman and he has lung cancer.

The reason why the photographer took this
photograph is to show how badly cigaretts
can hurt you and all the physical effects.
This man has no longer than a year to live.

Chim (girl), age 16

What scares me

what scares me is the thought of being taken away from my mother. or away from my family. or my mother being taken away from me. That scares me because I wouldNt and dont want it to happen. I love her so much that I cant bare to see my life without her. I really seriously dont know what I would do if she was gone. Death is what mainly scares me!

14

"What Scares Me"
Fear, Vulnerability, Aggression

I'm worried about going home 'cause I've been here for so long.
I'm worried I'll mess up again. It's just because the people
I live around in the neighborhood – I'm just worried about going home.

—**Sands** (girl), resident of GRF, Juvenile Hall

We entered GRF for what would turn out to be our final visit. Coach Mary greeted Polly and me. She talked about Sands, saying "She's gonna end up in an institution. She's very violent. But she's going home tomorrow."

We had met Sands's mother during an earlier visit. We knew she had her hands full with a daughter who acted older than her mother at times and switched to the behavior of a toddler at the slightest provocation. We had witnessed the range of Sands's reactions, from a nervous, frightened child exhibiting a lack of remorse all the way to a youth concerned about her feelings toward her mother, scared of her own inability to manage impulses. This awareness was progress, yet it was not enough for her to sustain a healthy pattern outside the Hall if she were released without support.

Sands was just one of many who desperately needed a close one-on-one relationship with a trustworthy individual. Sadly, most of these kids were as lost as Sands. They acted out, sometimes louder and louder, to test us and see if we would listen.

After a year of visits, the girls in GRF were treating us as regular features of the Hall; we were their listeners and sometimes their entertainers. They were learning from being with us. This was a very powerful experience for Polly and me to share. The more time we spent in the Hall, the more we realized how little we had known about kids inside Juvenile Hall.

We learned from the girls on over 40 occasions—and even from the boys, although in unit groups—that they wanted help. They knew they were not in treatment long enough to heal the sickness they felt deep inside, the sickness that impelled them toward more heinous acts. By this time in our journey with these girls we were feeling that they accepted us and we accepted them. Overwhelmed by their issues, they felt a connection to us because we cared enough to work with them patiently and listen to their troubles. In many ways, they were simply terrified little children.

Still, it was very important for us to maintain boundaries. When Sands was dismissed the first time, we were permitted to visit her at her home and take her for snack breaks to talk about school and her transition back into her neighborhood. We did not see her mother, however. Sands was home, alone. She was more disorganized in her thinking and she appeared negative about school, relationships, her family, and her neighborhood. She was depressed and often apathetic about being with us. It was easier to get a sense of her real personality while she was in the Hall. There, she moved in and out of negative thoughts and often laughed at herself and with others. It was a beautiful thing to see. But the visits to her home were concerning. It wasn't long after our last visit with her that she was returned to the Hall.

Children seem more vulnerable than adults to compulsive
behavioral repetition and loss of conscious memory of trauma.

–Bessel A. van der Kolk, M.D.
"The Compulsion to Repeat the Trauma"

> MY VERY FIRST MEMORY IS NOT A VERY POSITIVE ONE, IN FACT ITS NOT AT ALL SOMETHING THAT I CHOOSE TO REALLY RECALL AT ALL. THIS MEMORY TOOK PLACE BETWEEN THE AGES OF 3 OR 4 YEARS OF AGE. (I AM NOW 16)
>
> MY FIRST MEMORY IS ONE OF DOMESTIC VIOLENCE, BETWEEN MY TWO PARENTS. BOTH OF THEM BEING ALCOHOLICS, THEY DIDNT GET ALONG WELL DURING THIER TIMES OF INTOXICATION. (WHICH WAS VERY OFTEN)
>
> IN THE ALTERCATION THAT MY PARENTS WERE HAVING, I REMEMBER MY DAD HOLDING A KNIFE TO MY MOTHERS THROAT, & I RECALL MY MOM HOLDING A SHOT-GUN TO MY FATHERS HEAD.
>
> BUT I WOULD LIKE TO ADD THAT I BELIEVE THAT MY DISFUNCTIONAL FAMILY WAS NOT THE SOLE REASON FOR ME TURNING OUT THE WAY I HAVE. IVE HAD MANY OPPORTUNITIES TO BETTER MYSELF, BUT, AT THE TIME I WAS IGNORANT C TOOK THE EASY WAY OUT.

Lake (girl), age 15

We saw the fear and sometimes terror these youths felt when we attended sessions at the Juvenile Court of San Diego, another part of our mission. We had permission from the presiding judge for entry. Aware of our purpose and goal, he did not hesitate once he understood we had already worked with several of the kids and we respected the court's confidentiality requirement.

Our third morning in one of the courtrooms, a troubled 14-year-old boy stood before the tough-minded judge. The judge said, "Next time you'll do nine years. You hear, kid? I'm on your side..."

Observing the youth, we could see that he was frozen in space and had to be ushered out of the courtroom with a bailiff's hand on his back. They disappeared out the back of the courtroom to the corridor connecting the courthouse with the Hall.

It was hard to fathom exactly what he was feeling. Sullen, silent, and most likely furious inside, he scuffed along, handcuffed and shackled, through the long covered walkway and entered the backside of the Hall. Three coaches stood by, waiting—two in the Control Room and one ready to receive, pat down, and remove cuffs and shackles. He would be escorted to a boys' unit for kids who commit assaults. Such youths sent to the Hall hit the cold walls and harsh reality of lockup. The coaches rush around, as Sands had stated, "buzzing around but not connecting." Now I understood what she meant when we followed this teen from the court to the Hall.

While sitting in the courtroom, Polly and I witnessed other kids returning to the court for having violated probation. These kids were angry. One could see a sense of entitlement. They were seasoned. Reentering the Hall would be yet another experience, unlike the first visit. There may be a profound opportunity to help a youth incarcerated for the first time. However, the expression on the face of a youth standing before a judge for the second or third time says a lot: The judge is merely another authority figure among the many the youth has experienced. The judge has a thankless job.

In adult courtrooms everywhere, similar attitudes exist among those sentenced to prison, yet the public welcomes lockup for adults who break the laws of society. Children such as Sands, having lost the opportunity to grow, be nurtured, and change, reenter the juvenile justice system with tainted attitudes and impulses. Their situations reveal entirely different and complex sets of circumstances.

We gathered in the conference room once again. Coach Mary told us Anderson was probably out on El Cajon Boulevard prostituting. Sands energetically entered the conference room informing us she was not going home. I handed her an architectural book to peruse. Hui entered. Polly told them we were going to talk about spaces pertaining to photos I had taken. Hui sat down, quite businesslike, and took the book on the famous architect, I. M. Pei. Sands started talking openly.

> **Sands**: Because I threw my water bottle and hit the wall I got into trouble. I throw hard. I was sitting in a chair and we were having group.
> **Susan**: What I'd like to have you do today is draw your room from wherever you want to be sitting in the room—a perspective. [I illustrate from an image inside one of the books.]
> **Hui**: I really can't do that.
> **Sands**: Can I draw a pile of shit? OK if I draw a window and some barbed wire?

Chim asked good questions about perspective. She was interested. Minton listened but looked dazed. Something was wrong with Hui. I touched Sands's hand; she was cold. And worried.

> **Sands**: I'm not leaving the Hall.
> **Minton**: When are you going home?
> **Sands**: Never.
> **Hui**: You know what's foul is that people even come after me get released first. That's really foul. Plus the people who come in after me get sentenced first. I really don't appreciate that. I don't like the judges here. They're really kinky.

Polly: Did you see I. M. Pei? One of the most successful architects in the world, Asian, and responsible for some of the most glorious architecture.

Hui: *The Wizard of Oz* is in my room.

Sands: That book makes me mad. Because he's mean to the tree. The tree's giving and he's selfish. He needs to die.

Chim: So that's called the Giving Tree. He'll die on that stump.

Hui: It's something you should learn a lesson from because people are too nice... And other people take advantage.

Chim: That's true. That's why I'm becoming my old self again.

Minton: You know you've been a little bitch to me lately.

Susan: Who has been a little bitch?

Minton: Hui.

Hui: Don't be calling me a little bitch. I don't appreciate that.

Sands: I'm worried about going home 'cause I've been here for so long. I'm worried I'll mess up again. It's just because the people I live around in the neighborhood—I'm just worried about going home. I'm just worried about coming back and violating probation.

As Diane Campbell often told us, "Being attached is too dangerous." They fear it. The girls were confused and often spoke of depression and anger towards the staff.

Hui: I wanna go home.

Coach Mary came in and said family was in the waiting room; there could be no more "kill her" or Sands wouldn't leave tomorrow.

Susan: What does "kill her" mean?

Chim: Let me kill her.

Sands: I fucking hate that coach. See how they fuck with me? Tomorrow might never come. You're the only ones who talk to us appropriately and give us respect. The other ones don't.

Hui: You come here on your own time.

Polly: Does it help to see us?

Chim: Yeah it does. I can't let my feelings out to anybody because if I even use a word profanity it would start trouble here.

Minton: I love you both.

Sands: Can I say something! Don't try to copy my answer.

Minton: I didn't copy your answer.

Polly: Ok. Let's talk about beliefs. Minton, what's your perception of god?

Minton: The god I have faith in. Jesus.

Hui: My god is Buddha. He means a lot of things. The five perceptions; the four noble truths.

Chim: I ask you what Buddha really means to you. It means the Enlightened One.

Susan: Would you pray to your god and hope for miracles?

Chim: I'd pray to my god and watch my back. Ha.

Hui: I have no idea. I never had that happen.

Susan: You never had anything dangerous happen to you?

Hui: No.

Susan: Well, you landed in here.

Hui: That's nothing dangerous!

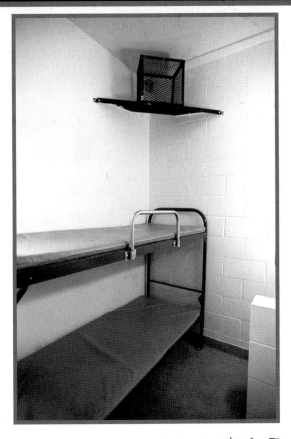

a cell. a lonely place. a place to think
of your regrets, a place where your tears
speak. Your eyes want to see the sun, moon, stars.
The place where you talk to god. you discipline
and learn your lesson. A place where some people
Deserve to be. yet some people dont. YouR
sadness, your fear, your madness, insaneness,
tears, come out. some people have no feeling
or thoughts. spend a short or long time a
place were you hope. I feel I can do better
in life, this isn't where I need to be.
I need to follow my dreams. not spend
my time in here. I pray everyday in my
cell. I think, remember, learn, want, cry,
see things I don't want to see but that's
the same thing outside of here except I'm
being locked in a box wondering to god
what will happen. My dream is to do
something with photography also. I will
fullfill that outside of here

Langdon (girl), age 14

East Mesa Juvenile Detention Facility – San Diego, CA

Susan: That was a pretty scary time, wasn't it?

Hui: I still hate that person who I robbed. I have hate for her big time. I wanna shoot her. I can't stand scandalous people. Especially Playa haters.

Polly: What does scandalous mean to you?

Hui: Stupid ignorant people who are just scandalous. Who are whores...they act like one, look like one, go around sleeping with other people's husbands, they take people's money. Wanting to call the cops on people. I hate scandalous people like that.

Polly: You feel you're helping god out by taking care of these scandalous people?

Hui: I really don't care.

Chim: I'm not helping god. I'm helping other people.

Hui: I really don't care. The reason...how'd you feel if...someone said you stole her husband. Someone else has fought for her and she should learn her lesson by now 'cause I don't appreciate her going around talking "smack" about my mom.

> Someone killed my grandfather...what goes around comes around. I'm gonna go kill somebody else's grandfather.
>
> —**Hui** (girl), age 15

Susan: That's pretty, Sands. You could use that as a border for stationary. What do you think about taking control over something you don't agree with?

Chim: Now I know what she's mad about.

Sands: They just buzz, they don't back their shit up...they just buzz. They just strut. They pack shit but they walk away like lizards.

Chim: What I also don't like is when people say they'll do something and then they don't. They get on my nerves.

Polly: Sit back for two seconds. Take a deep breath.

Hui: I'm really pissed off.

Sands: Damn, you can draw pretty good.

Minton is creating a Valentine.

Hui: I'm really frustrated.

Polly: Minton, you're quiet. What are you thinking of?

Minton: I'd just rather be home. I was supposed to be home. They don't want me to be with my sister in National City because I've been up there for so long and they don't think she can handle me. And then my grandma had another stroke. She's been under a lot of stress. And then my aunt because she lives in my neighborhood and my cousin... Last time I got out I lived in our neighborhood but now it's a problem.

Sands: They buzza. Buzz-a. Bees can talk all their shit but all they do is hit the door.

Hui: They can fly but when they get to buzzing...it's the way to talk. They have nothing to back it up so when they start flying they hit the door.

Susan: Boredom is an issue with you.

Sands: I get bored very easily. That's what I'm worried about because I go home and I get bored and I have personal weed I smoke by myself or my friends...and I get bored and I'm not gonna do that.

She faked a throwing a pen. I jerked.

Sands: Why'd you flinch? Did you think I was going to throw it?

Hui talked fast. She attacked Minton's lack of confidence in her work. She was upset that Minton didn't share Hui's standard of excellence in work. Yet the structure and values of Hui's moral life were entirely different. Hui didn't see the seriousness of her crime, as she was still immersed in the relationship with her brothers and family, her "lost soul of the U.S.A." stuff. She was sharp yet she kept insisting, "Nothing is perfect; nothing is right."

Susan: You talk about wanting to kill someone to get back at those who killed your grandfather.
Hui: One thousand... I already understand that. I already had my family members taken from me so I might as well go do that. Kill 1,000.

Polly: What family members?
Hui: I had my *brothers* taken away. They're locked up in there.
Sands: Because they did something.

Susan: So they were not taken from you. They were irresponsible. They're living in a country that has a different set of values.
Hui: Why are we in here? I don't like the Hall. I hope all the staff in here dies.

Polly: I think you're feeling a lot of pain about your loss.
Hui: What goes around comes around.
Sands: We already got it coming around 'cause we're in here.
Hui: Someone killed my grandfather...what goes around comes around. I'm gonna go kill somebody else's grandfather.

Susan: How long ago was that?
Hui: Ten or 11 years ago. My dad's dad.

Polly: In America?
Hui: No, it wasn't in America, but I really don't care 'cause they're all humans.

Susan: Hui, you're living in a civilization that has tremendous respect for education and fairness towards one another. This is something that happened a long time ago in another country.
Hui: But I really will go back to that country and kill somebody who killed my grandfather. Actually I kind of have an idea who it is.

Polly: When you get into "I'm gonna go kill blah, blah..." That sounds like a lot of big, bad attitude.
Hui: I will.

Susan: I don't think that's who you are.
Hui: I've had enough of "Oh Hui, she's a nice Hui." I hate sucking up.
Chim: Then why do you do it?

Polly: You have some culture and education behind you.
Hui: That's really a lie 'cause I don't have any behind me. I only have... Even a little girl is smarter than me.

Susan: You're in a self-pity mode.

Sands burped, then spoke.

Questionnaire: RC
boys night 1

Packet Number:

Initials:
Unit: 900
Age: 15

1) Is this your first time being in Juvenile Hall? If not, how many times have your been there? Twice This is my second time

---

Questionnaire: RC
boys night 1

Packet Number:

Initials:
Unit: 900
Age: 15

1) Is this your first time being in Juvenile Hall? If not, how many times have your been there? a lot

a) Is Juvenile Hall like you thought it would be? Why/why not?
because I thought it Would be hard.

b) When you get out of Juvenile Hall what would you like to accomplish for other young people so they don't have to experience Juvenile Hall?
Just tall them ~~to~~ don't let anyone
see you

---

dont FORGET ME

Questionnaire: RC
boys night 1

Packet Number: 7

Initials:
Unit: 1200
Age: 16

1) Is this your first time being in Juvenile Hall? If not, how many times have your been there? 5 TIMES. BUT I CANT help it NO MORE

a) Is Juvenile Hall like you thought it would be? Why/why not?
YES i DID BECAUSE now THEY TRWT You.

b) When you get out of Juvenile Hall what would you like to accomplish for other young people so they don't have to experience Juvenile Hall?
TELL THEM to BE good KID AND DONT COME
HERE

Questionnaire: RC
boys night 1

Packet Number: 33

Initials:
Unit: 1200
Age: 17

1) Is this your first time being in Juvenile Hall? If not, how many times have you been there? No? a lot, about 20 something times, estimation

a) Is Juvenile Hall like you thought it would be? Why/why not? No? Because I
thought it would be a lot harder then it is.
And it would look a lot more worse than it does.
b) When you get out of Juvenile Hall what would you like to accomplish for other young people so they don't have to experience Juvenile Hall? I would like
to go to the navey so I would be able to start my own
boys & girls club and tell them about what I've
been through so they would know not to get
into trouble

Sands: Excuse me. Hui, I don't appreciate you sitting here and feeling sorry for yourself and you have the intelligence you have!

Susan: I think you are frustrated about your culture now. Write about that.

Hui: I really don't want to be in this country. I'd rather be in my mom's country smoking weed where it's legal. My brother shared something else with me. When I get mad I don't forgive and forget easily. If I forgive I don't forget. My first impression is not always smiles.

Hui's angry sensitivity about what others think of her illustrates an important point. Psychological researcher Geraldine Downey and her colleagues have demonstrated that people who anxiously expect negative responses from others have more fragile relationships, perceive rejection in ordinary behavior, respond to conflict and rejection in ways that undermine their relationships, become less engaged, and do less well in their academic institutions over time. Chim's earlier comment about education resonated with this point as well: "I'd like to go to college but I don't think I can… School is hard for me."

Many of these frightened, aggressive, and vulnerable youths have never experienced nurturing, let alone unconditional love, or even normal human responses; therefore, they're not capable of loving. How can we expect them to react humanly, with empathy, when they have never had a real taste of humanity?

Uneducated or ignorant parents with addictions or a history of abuse cannot serve their children well. They and their children are suffering from abuse, neglect, and trauma. As Diane Campbell noted, "When a little girl whose parents were killed in a car accident says, 'The most horrible thing to happen is my aunt wouldn't let me eat ice cream before dinner,' it shows a frightening lack of empathy." And without appropriate and consistent intervention, generation after generation repeats this destructive cycle.

Many young women, victims of unresolved neglect, merely tolerate their lives by using drugs. Seeking love for themselves, they again give birth, when they're incapable of loving the infant. Then, because of sick relationships involving abuse and power and street drugs, they leave these babies for society to pick up and cradle.

But our social delivery systems for providing that cradle, some kind of parental substitutes, are often competing for funds and unable to make the right decisions about how to tackle the issues at hand. With probation funds being stripped in many cities and officers' jobs being cut, we are losing three generations of children. They are falling into serious drug use to numb their pain. They cannot possibly understand how to conquer their emotional deficits and their addictions without help and supervision. In our final chapter, we outline actions that we believe can help.

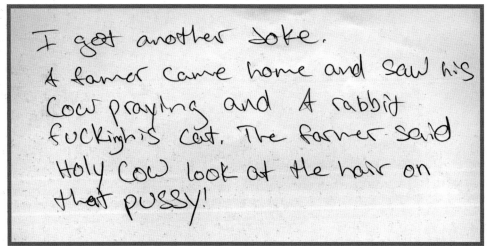

I get another joke.
A farmer came home and saw his cow praying and A rabbit fucking his cat. The farmer said Holy cow look at the hair on that pussy!

Carter (boy), age 16

This dog reminds me off my own dog coco. She's off to work at the gas station on an everyday thing. The damn dog stinks too. The picture looks like she's breaking out of my house like she does everyday If I could catch that damn dog but She always gets away from me. This dog also eats any thing that fucking moves. I was with my dog one night my friend droped a bagged of speed and my dog ate that Shit up. That fucking dog was tweeking out of her mind She was running circles around me all night. I think that wacked out dog even ate a cat. I felt like shit after that and never did that again.

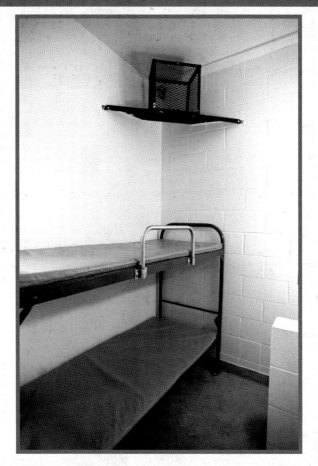

I see sadness. I see a hard life. I see my life, I see this won't be my life after my baby is born becouse I haft to change for my baby. I dont whont my baby to grow up like me. If I'm not in here my baby is going to have the best life in the whole world

15

If They Had a Raft
A Call to Action

If they had a raft, if they had a river, there'd be a song.
They'd sing of the joy in their hearts,
their wishes and wants to please others.
They'd talk of building friendships and getting education.
They'd laugh about a dirty joke and look up
"screw and fuck" in the dictionary.
If there were a raft.

"Screw and fuck" come along with guns,
with probation violations and family in the pen
where "screw and fuck" are real.
"Fuck you" and "get screwed."

Their voices echo:
You asked me about a god before.
I have a god. He tells me what to do.
You asked me about my wants and desires before.
I don't have any.
You asked me what I want to do in ten years.
How should I know? I don't know if I'll be alive.

We've asked for the raft and we're offered the cell.
We dream of the river and we're shown the sea.
It's too big to swim across.
"Do it anyway!" we are told.
"Fuck you. I'm screwed," we say.
Something needs to change.

After one year of visiting the youths at the Hall, Polly and I received notice that we were no longer welcome. A new director was arriving and she didn't want us in the Hall. Glares, stares, and silent smiles said the rest. I visited with County Supervisor Ron Roberts to see if we could extend our work in the Hall and met with resistance. Along with the new director would come a new set of rules.

It was one thing for us to be through with our visits. We clearly had enough material to understand the complexities of answering our initial question—"How did these kids get into this mess?" However, the kids—particularly the girls in GRF—looked forward to our visits. We looked forward to seeing them as well. There was a remarkable reunion each time we met in the small conference room, each time wondering what little or big crisis in their lives they might want to share. By the end of each session, they were softened, wearing warm expressions, and we sensed they would make a peaceful transition into the next day. Limited as our contact was, it was real. It felt sustaining for Polly and me.

We were allowed no closure, no opportunity to let the kids know why we no longer would be visiting the Hall. We did not relish the fact that we, too, were leaving them, as everyone else had left them or would leave them. Leaving them to whom? Sharp educators, sensitive counselors, parental replacements—or the grimmer reality of inconsistent institutional supervision?

In no way did we feel we were the answer. Yet we were getting too close to give up on finding solutions. When I returned to pick up the remainder of the girls' contributions, Hui saw me and ran up with a hug. "Susie, I miss you and Polly so much. Why aren't you coming anymore?"

Because we weren't clergy, HIV counselors, programmed researchers, or random substitute teachers, the kids were willing to risk sharing. We were something else. That something else was not intentional; it evolved. They became a part of our lives, not because we felt responsible for them, but simply because we were there.

We had learned about the vast differences between the so-called "eight percenters"—the persistent, intractable delinquents—and the other 92 percent, those who may be locked up for a first offense or for multiple probation violations, the youths who carry the potential to turn their lives around. In the adult prison setting, the "eight percenters" are responsible for using 80 percent of the resources. Many perceive that the same ratio exists in the Hall. With young people in particular, it's the 92 percent who could truly

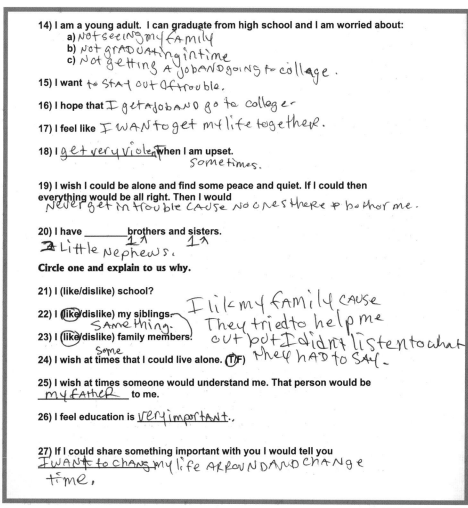

14) I am a young adult. I can graduate from high school and I am worried about:
   a) Not seeing my family
   b) Not graduating in time
   c) Not getting a job and going to collage.

15) I want to stay out of trouble.

16) I hope that I get a job and go to college.

17) I feel like I want to get my life together.

18) I get very violent when I am upset. Sometimes.

19) I wish I could be alone and find some peace and quiet. If I could then everything would be all right. Then I would Never get in trouble cause no ones there to bother me.

20) I have _____ brothers and sisters. 1   1
   A Little Nephews.

Circle one and explain to us why.

21) I (like/dislike) school?

22) I (like/dislike) my siblings. Same thing.) I like my family cause
   They tried to help me
23) I (like/dislike) family members! out but I didnt listen to what
   Some
24) I wish at times that I could live alone. (T/F) they had to say.

25) I wish at times someone would understand me. That person would be my father to me.

26) I feel education is very important..

27) If I could share something important with you I would tell you I want to change my life around and change time.

Love (boy), age 15

benefit if resources were devoted to proven interventions. As Bruce Perry has pointed out, locking them up in a facility may simply send them on their way to Ph.D. degrees in criminal behavior. The financial cost and the moral cost to society is far more expensive than prevention.

"We don't have them in the Hall long enough to educate them," probation officers told us over and over. "They come and go." Exactly, they come and they go with relative ease. And we, as a society, need to figure out a way to smooth their paths, both inside and out.

Many youthful offenders, like Sands, "sabotage" their exits. The Hall represents safety. They fantasize about a new life on the outside, but in reality the outside represents a form of chaos as they try desperately to fight off their addictions and other aberrant tendencies. The plain fact is they will go back to the same old thing. Trying to find love, trying to establish a new pattern, only to be confronted with the old standards and the odds stacked against them. Sands returned while we were in the Hall. She returned trying to show attitude, but she was clearly happy to be back. She felt good about herself in the little conference room.

There were so many facets to what we witnessed and to the lovingly desperate characters we met in the Hall. It's obvious that we as a society have failed them. Their mothers and fathers are adults with teenage minds, still reacting impulsively like teenagers. Or they come from faraway cultures, some of which, like Cambodia, have a recent history of violent genocide. Many refugee families, already traumatized in their home countries, have no understanding of what it takes to live and work in America. So how could their children? The culture and class issues present very complicated challenges.

---

4) Do you have a positive role model that you can talk to?

I look up to my Dad. He's my best friend. Although, talking to him can be hard.

5) Do you have any family members that have been, or are in jail or prison?

Yes, not really family that I like or am close to.

6) What are your plans for the future?

Finish school, go to Palomar college, and get my EMT. Become a fireman/paramedic.

7) What have you given deep thought to since you have been in Juvenile Hall?

My family. How much I love them, and how much I miss them. Also my past. NO MORE tagging.

8) If you have one wish to change something in your life, what would it be?

Change my record. Not something to be proud of. Without this, everything would be cool.

9) Remember when you used to dream as a small child. What did you want to be when you grew up?

A Fireman. That's what my dad is. One Day, it WILL happen.

10) Have you ever been subjected to peer pressure? If so, how did it make you feel? How would you change it if you could and why?

Not really. I always did what I wanted to. IF someone told me to do something, I did it because I wanted to. Not because they told me to.

11) What was your most memorable event (in your past)?

Going to Canada with my dad. (Twice) Snowboarding and hangin out, I'll never forget it.

12) Do you feel your contribution can help kids stay out of trouble? If not, what

Actually, NO. Kids are going to do what they want to regardless of what anyone says or does. It is the truth.

Gordon (boy), age 15

This photograph makes me feel sad. The man in this picture looks meloncholly and hopeless. This guys expression seems to describe how I've spent most of my life feeling. At the same time, he looks as though his eyes are reaching out to the person looking at the photograph, asking them for help, or a chance at life. The photographer has captured much feeling in this photograph.

Photo by John Ramsey Miller © John Ramsey Miller   Reese (girl), age 16

Immature parents have babies who then have babies. Gangs continue to spread at a cancerous rate. Individuals who turn to gangs as surrogate families do not develop into productive, tax-paying citizens. Youths with such disrupted parenting—and underdeveloped brains—have no idea what constitutes a normal life.

Institutions like Juvenile Hall are not a good substitute for family. "The branch is cut off from the tree. A twig out there by itself can't survive," says Diane Campbell. The youths in the Hall don't need miracle workers; they simply need someone who is "just good enough." But how will they find that someone when the staff—coaches, teachers, therapists, directors—rotate frequently? Polly and I had witnessed the disruptive power of departmental politics on several occasions. Now we ourselves were being booted out by the military-style detention director replacing Sara.

We left the Hall needing to do something to help stop the madness of locking kids up in lieu of focusing on improving their abilities and behavior. We spent months attending child-abuse conferences, meeting neuroscientists with the latest on the effects of trauma and abandonment on the lives of little American citizens, and talking to politicians.

Although change is crucial within the walls of the Hall, we came to recognize that true solutions begin outside, where we as a society can have the greatest impact. If we educate ourselves and then act—with our voices, our votes, our checkbooks, and our time—we can all help make a difference.

One of the experts we spoke to was Amy Lansing, a neuropsychologist who has worked with young people in the Hall. "There's a sea of kids who need help in the community before they get into the justice system," she told us. "If we can effect change and we do it early, that's our best bet."

Another enlightening conversation was with psychiatrist Thomas Jensen, an expert on bipolar and other disorders. He stressed the importance of early detection of emotional and psychological conditions, and lamented that careful evaluation and treatment often isn't available to at-risk youth, particularly those who land in juvenile facilities. "No one ever developed a work ethic and sense of competence by focusing primarily on their weaknesses," he said.

Education in its traditional role is key. The majority of youths in Juvenile Hall perform below grade level in reading and math, and many are illiterate. School districts in our lower-income communities often lack the initiative to employ excellent teachers, which contributes to the cycle of delinquency. But our educational system must serve the needs of young people on another level, too, and create a full circle.

- Prenatal education and early parenting education should be available to women of all ages.

- Preschool educators and caregivers should be trained to identify behaviors that are disruptive to other children.

- Kindergarten teachers need guidelines for identifying children with regressive behaviors.

- By the time children reach fourth grade, many basic behavior patterns are secured; well-adjusted children can create, imagine, read, and socialize readily. Teachers at this level in particular must learn to recognize children at risk.

- Educators at all levels should recognize derailments. Attention to the signs may prevent a youth from further regression.

- Youths who have little family support need educators to refer them to advocacy organizations. In the case of abuse, Child Protective Services.

- To address the cycle of dysfunction, parenting classes should be offered in high schools as well as juvenile facilities. Learning about childhood developmental struggles might deter teens from taking a chance on pregnancy. At a minimum, these classes would educate young people who are already parents.

James Heckman, economist and Nobel laureate, has done tremendous work in the area of human potential, and speaks with authority about the economic gains of investing in childhood development. Heckman stresses the importance of the malleable early years neglected by social policy, of noncognitive social skills before cognitive achievement. His "Heckman Equation" offers a template for developing America's most precious resource—its people—and reducing crime in the process.

It's a tough challenge to change the mold. Probation has been about detention and not diversion. Without funding for valuable programs to remediate and educate our youths, we are merely providing good language to an insidious chancre—locking up youths and teaching them the tools for learned helplessness, more criminal behavior, and disrespect for authority.

As this book goes to print, a debate is raging in California and echoing across the country. Due in part to the budget crisis, the Department of Juvenile Justice, formerly the California Youth Authority, is undergoing reorganization and may turn over the supervision of youthful felons to the state's already overtaxed counties.

The proposal is highly controversial. If the DJJ were to close down, says psychiatrist Igor Koutsenok, more kids would be tried as adults. Also, without adequate funding of county Departments of Probation, high-risk youth could end up at even higher risk. On the other hand, long-time critics of the DJJ such as the Ella Baker Center, an Oakland-based civil rights organization, believe that the return of supervision to local authorities would lead to more humane treatment and more effective rehabilitation of young offenders.

However the debate resolves, this is an excellent opportunity for California and other states to examine what does and doesn't work in the realm of juvenile justice. Organizations such as the Missouri Juvenile Justice Association (MJJA) are taking the lead in promoting true justice and seeking effective reform.

Many other admirable nonprofits and governmental programs, large and small, are striving as well to address the challenges of juvenile justice and shift the focus from detention to diversion or rehabilitation. Bureaucracy, budget shortfalls, and inertia all create persistent roadblocks to accomplishing real change—all the more reason for individual citizens to be aware of these organizations and support them in whatever way we can.

- The Annie E. Casey Foundation's Juvenile Detention Alternatives Initiative (JDAI) strives to increase opportunities for youth in the juvenile-justice system, and has been implemented at over 100 sites in 30 states.

- The Mac Arthur Foundation's Models for Change: Systems Reform in Juvenile Justice program is committed to accelerating reform of juvenile-justice systems in selected states across the country.

- The National Center for School Engagement in Denver provides models for creating and assessing truancy reduction. Truancy is a major contributor to early delinquent patterns.

- Facilities such as Rainbow Lake School in Georgia blend outdoor activity and responsibility with traditional education and treatment.

- Youth Advocate Programs (YAP) and similar organizations offer effective and cost-efficient alternatives to the incarceration of young people.

An approach we heard about repeatedly was that of evidence-based programs and services, tailored to each child's needs and risks. As psychiatrist Igor Koutsenok told us, "These offenders are like patients who suffer a chronic condition. It is very complex and requires multiple services using the case management model—as in medicine." Psychiatrist Bruce Perry and San Diego's Chief Probation Officer Mack Jenkins agreed that society must put aside its demand for revenge through punishment, particularly for young people. Because punishment is not a deterrent, the juvenile-justice system must offer appropriate services that help change behavior. When these services are offered, the results are very encouraging.

Dr. Amy Lansing also agreed on the value of evidence-based interventions. She mentioned several

Every child

tools that were affordable and therefore appropriate, including Fast ForWord, an educational brain-fitness program; Seeking Safety, a cognitive-behavioral therapy for PTSD and addiction; and Adaptive Disclosure, which promotes early disclosure of traumatic memories.

"The further down the stream you go," she told us, "the greater the psychopathology, the greater the family adversity; these will be the kids who end up penetrating the juvenile-justice system further. At each farther stage in the system, you've got increasingly poor, increasingly minority kids, with increasingly high levels of learning disability, mental illness, everything."

Ideally, evidence-based programs would be implemented both in and out of Juvenile Hall. A child who leaves the juvenile-justice system still unable to read and still shaky in his or her recovery from drug addiction is highly unlikely to become engaged by school and to sustain positive change on the outside.

Heckman stresses the importance of the malleable early years neglected by social policy, of noncognitive social skills before cognitive achievement. His "Heckman Equation" offers a template for developing America's most precious resource—its people—and reducing crime in the process.

More innovative approaches for helping our young people show great promise, as well. Interacting with animals can strengthen empathy pathways for troubled youths who are resistant to adult supervision. They then learn to transfer that caring and sharing to humans. Connecting all young people, particularly in urban areas, to nature can aid in fostering the respect so critical to developing empathy. Work in community and school gardens offers one path toward this connection—as well as healthier eating habits.

For many of these interventions, whether it's planting tomatoes or improving reading skills, volunteers can play a powerful role. Because parents are so often an unlikely source of help, and because schools and the justice system so often "kick the ball farther down the road between institutions," as Lansing says, steady, stable, personal sources of support are crucial for at-risk kids. Though clearly the best time to help is before the child enters the justice system, such connection even afterward can make a difference, as Polly and I discovered from our own experience.

Our troubled youths would benefit greatly from the growth of a professional and responsible local volunteer base of great Americans willing to step up and commit their time and compassion. In many cultures, a "swarm" of family and community members pitch in to care for children. We cannot buy a swarm, but we can volunteer to be part of one. Retired Americans in particular have so much to offer—their wide-ranging professional experience leaves them well-equipped to help at-risk kids learn skills that will help them navigate the storms of life. Programs such as Senior Corps' Foster Grandparents are springing up to facilitate this natural collaboration.

is born innocent.

I was born on 2,11, at 11:00 am
my dad was not thery Just my
mom. my dad was in Jail
my Just got out we
moved to san diego when
I was 3 Year's ould my
mom got Lock up agine
I Lived with my Grand mom
in spring valley when I was
12 I got Jumped in to
spring valley I Put in
wonk I got shanked
fore time's that a Year
when I was 2/13 I seen
my home Boy R.i.P
die at that time I
whant to die to But
Life whent on I stared
doing Drug's a Lote one time
I was in the ~~hospily~~ hospytal
with a 50-50 chance to Live
at that point I was
coming in and out of
Jail

Jones (boy), age 16

my mom got out she did drug's agine so when I got out I did the same they my home Boy shorty RiP die I was all alone I felt I hade to kill that Bitch that kilea my home Boy's But my gruna mom ask me do you care if you Live or die I tould her I dont know still to this point I dont know I seen so meny home Boy's die ana every time I think it is going to Be my time Next Time

Jones (boy), age 16

There is so much to be concerned about with our young people, whether or not they've tangled with the juvenile-justice system. The number of mothers receiving early prenatal care is moving in the wrong direction. Obesity and truancy are both on the rise. Recent statistics on teen suicide are eye-opening and heartbreaking.

Drug and alcohol abuse in particular are a profound concern. Addiction underpins the neglect that so many of these young people experience in their families. Parental abuse of alcohol, peer influence, and hormonal changes can combine to push even a relatively normal youth into the danger zone.

Juvenile arrests for felonies are on the rise and misdemeanors are on the decline, which suggests that kids are taking bigger risks for more dangerous rewards. The uptick in felony arrests also reflects a lack of respect for personal property and lack of compassion for human and animal life. Every teen does a little something to assert his or her independence, but serious criminal behavior doesn't spring out of nowhere. A youth isn't an exemplary citizen today and a monster on a mission tomorrow.

Where are we as parents, siblings, teachers, clergy, coaches, and friends if we cannot bear witness to the trauma, abuse, and neglect that can ultimately evolve into criminal behavior? Why are we so tolerant of risky activities, and then so quick to say, "He's getting what he deserves," as the cops said to me the night four teens wrapped their car around a eucalyptus tree, all high on pot and booze?

Polly and I are now closer to answering our question, "How did these kids get into this mess?"

Through our work on this project, we learned the power of knowledge. We learned that parenting skills are critical to raising a strong, healthy, and happy child, one who is capable of flourishing and opening up creative links to his or her own future. We learned that bonding and nurturing contribute to the growth of less defensive and more empathetic youth; that adequate attachment also leads to the essential ability to respect and learn from elders and authority; and that a healthy sense of humor can ease tough decision-making for our children.

As a parent, it was often painful to watch my daughters grow up and leave the nest, but now that they've found their wings, now that they're free to live and learn, teach others, and enjoy relationships, I feel like I have it made. Life is beautiful. As a society, we can't afford to ignore those who are marginalized, stuck in the emptiness of poverty, family violence, abuse, or addiction. Together we must search for solutions so that a beautiful life is possible for all the children who are born into—and, when necessary, raised by—a caring larger society.

At last…

The raft has arrived. The chorus sings. The birds fly in formation.
And the youths walk in the breeze. Down the alleyway, the raft awaits.
Untrusting the loving hands aboard, youths fear they're freight;
not certain of their fate.
The task is ours to create; ours to ensure.
These youths, more than plenty, are unable to take oar.
Henry and Margaret sit alongside the shore.
They watch the youths submit and board.
Gleefully, sputtering sounds of surprise,
once they push away from rocks and dirt—is it merely surprise,
or will it stick and will they thrive?
The task is ours to create.

—Susan Madden Lankford

Afterword

Criminal behavior has always been a focus of the age-old debate between nature and nurture. Is it the responsibility of an individual's genetic makeup that makes them a criminal or is it the environment in which they are raised that determines their outcome? Are you destined from birth to become ruthless and cold-hearted? Is it the parents' fault for raising their children poorly?

Many people have been trying to determine when a human can be identified as a criminal, so that criminality can be prevented, deterred, or even reversed. Research has been conducted regarding this debate, which has resulted in the conclusion that both genes and environment do play a role in the development of criminal behavior of an individual. However, very limited progress has been made, due to there being no realistic way to conduct conclusive experiments. Various studies have shown that twins split apart at birth will have similar characteristics, especially in the areas of aggressiveness, nurturance, empathy, and assertiveness. Obviously this shows that we are born with some innate personality traits, which leads me to believe that becoming a criminal is not a matter of nature versus nurture, but rather an issue of nature and nurture in accordance with each other. By this I mean that although anyone can potentially become a criminal, people who are born with such personality traits as high impulsivity with aggressive tendencies are much more likely to commit crimes if they have had an abnormal upbringing.

Those who support the nature side of the argument claim that personality is natural, and that you inherit behaviors due to various interactions of genes. For example, if your mother was easily annoyed, and your father was easily annoyed, then you will most likely share that same characteristic. This might be true, and it certainly looks as if something genetic is going on since this characteristic runs in families. Well, English speaking runs in most families in the U.S. as well, but common sense tells me that it would be very hard to consider this trend as being genetic. Even if it were, genetic tendencies unfold in a social context, which definitely should be considered in analyzing a behavior as complex as criminality. In fact, family dynamics have been found critical to the upbringing of a child, and if problems exist then the child is most likely to suffer the consequences. The science identifies family risk factors as poverty, education, parenting practices, and family structure. Families with poor communication and weak family bonds have been shown to have a correlation with children's development of aggressive/criminal behavior. Another indicator of future antisocial or criminal behavior is that of abuse or neglect in childhood. There is compelling research evidence that children are at a 50 percent greater risk of engaging in criminal acts if they were neglected or abused. This has been one of the most popular arguments as to why children develop antisocial or delinquent behaviors. Many other environmental influences have been studied and found important in forming criminal behavior as well.

So, the discussion "Born or Raised?" relevant to criminality has a very long history, is still ongoing, and most likely will not stop in our lifetime. Why? Because both arguments are partially true.

Let me remind you of a story of six blind men who were asked to determine what an elephant looked like by touching the animal. The blind man who feels a leg says the elephant is like a pillar; the one who feels the tail says the elephant is like a rope; the one who feels the trunk says the elephant is like a tree branch; the one who feels the ear says the elephant is like a hand fan; the one who feels the belly says the elephant is like a wall; and the one who feels the tusk says the elephant is like a solid pipe.

The question is, are they wrong? Not at all. They just describe a part of the story, based on their perception and research. So we can get a total picture of the elephant by putting all of the perspectives together, and this will resolve the conflict. This story illustrates the principle of living in harmony with people who have different belief systems, and that truth can be stated in different ways.

Born, Not Raised presents the truth by offering multiple perspectives, and this I think is the beauty of Susan Lankford's work.

—Igor Koutsenok, M.D., M.S.
University of California San Diego, Department of Psychiatry

Appendix

A Gallery of Feelings, Drawings, Dreams

Born, Not Raised provides an important look into the reality for large segments of our young population, the reality of broken lives many Americans never know exist nor really care to know.

The themes reflected in this gallery offer a framework for understanding the emotional valence that permeates the lives of youth in Juvenile Hall: domestic violence, restricted opportunities, incarceration as an expected outcome across generations of families, health disparities, abandonment, and fear that life for them will be short. Despite all this, many "high risk" youths feel a longing for connection.

Susan Madden Lankford and Polly Lankford Smith created a unique opportunity to engage these young people. Arrested and detained youth typically interact with adults who are assigned to manage their behavior: social workers who might remove them from their homes, police who might arrest them, and correctional officers who have the authority to direct and monitor their movement, daily habits, and conversations. The youths represented in these pages rose to the challenges presented by Polly and Susan—to stretch their minds and consider other possibilities (e.g., college) and to provide their opinions and insights on a variety of topics (photography, literature, family). The sheer variety of relatively unstructured opportunities to write, think, or talk one-on-one or in small groups allowed these youths to drop their guard and reach out to form connections with the visiting women and with their fellow detainees. The revealing results arose from their rare opportunity to talk openly and without censor to adults who were genuinely interested in what they thought about, what their lives were like, and what their aspirations were. These young people demonstrate exquisite vulnerability. Their responses reflect heartbreak, trauma, loss, isolation, and beliefs that range from a yearning for connection to a profound absence of hope. Some view their lives as a devastating void where no positive outcomes can even be imagined.

The pervasiveness of the problem becomes a harsh reality when over two million youths are arrested in the U.S. annually. Each young person who drops out of school and continues a life of crime costs society an estimated $2.6 to $3.1 million in their lifetime (adjusted for 2009 relative-dollar value). A substantial portion of these costs result from functional impairments associated with direct and indirect exposure to trauma as well as deficits in educational, occupational, and social competence. These deficits become amplified and more intractable as these youths age and as developmental and societal demands increase. Further, many youths with the most severely impairing psychiatric disorders and significant trauma histories are never seen in traditional mental health service venues.

Detained youths represent an extremely underserved population seen primarily through Juvenile

Court, which provides the umbrella for both Child Welfare and the Juvenile Justice system. Researchers estimate that 67 to 75 percent of delinquent youths have a mental disorder, with 20 percent having severe mental disorders, and greater than one-third needing ongoing mental health service care—a figure twice the rate of the general adolescent population. Notably, rates of posttraumatic stress disorder in delinquent youths are up to eight times higher than in community youths. Despite legal mandates, detained youths are a profoundly underserved population. Prospective data on juvenile detainees with major mental illness suggest only 15 percent received treatment during detention and 8 percent received treatment in the community. The level of need is particularly dire for girls, who appear to have not only exceptionally high rates of mental disorders, but the most significant childhood maltreatment histories.

The complexity of the problem is further illuminated by current research on neurocognitive deficits and behavioral functioning among adults with psychopathology, which suggests that a deep understanding of cognition may be key to designing treatment programs for delinquent youths. Specifically, these studies find that neurocognitive deficits continue to predict functional impairment even when psychiatric symptoms are ameliorated. This is an important point because data suggest that delinquents not only have high rates of mental illness but also have significant neurocognitive deficits relative to nondelinquents—particularly when delinquency begins early and persists through adolescence and beyond.

Despite financial, sentencing, and policy fluctuations over time, the goal of the juvenile-justice system, unlike our adult system, remains rehabilitation. Alternatives to detention are sorely needed—especially for mentally ill, substance-using, and neurologically impaired individuals—yet criminal-justice reform alone is too narrow a focus. We must advocate for social change, and address directly the cumulative disadvantage that contributes to vulnerable families and fragile neighborhoods. Criminal-justice policies cannot be responsible for addressing health disparities, low performing schools, inadequate resources, untreated mental illness (including substance and alcohol abuse), belief systems that support mass incarceration of large segments of our society, and a lack of healthy opportunities for individuals who do not fit neatly into normative expectations. We must broaden our scope, "listen to" the dire circumstances reflected by the children within these pages, and aspire to social policies that will enhance the lives of all.

When the author of this revealing book invited me to provide comments on some of the contributions of the young people she interviewed in Juvenile Hall, I was honored to do so. This commentary appears in the pages that follow.

—Amy Lansing, Ph.D.
Assistant Professor
Department of Psychiatry, School of Medicine
University of California, San Diego

It is impossible not to be struck by the cogent themes expressed by these youths: cross-generational incarceration, familial substance abuse and the sense of being a lost soul, irrevocably damaged, isolated, and set adrift.

It is important to underscore that often the criminal behavior demonstrated by these youths is behavior that they engage in with their parents, at their parents' request, or with their parents' knowledge. Punishing children through incarceration—without understanding the broader context (family, neighborhoods, etc.) and appreciating that addiction and its consequences crosses socioeconomic lines—is both ineffective and naive.

—Amy Lansing, Ph.D.

this lady looks as if she's frustrated. she looks as if she also thinking of what's going on on the otherside of the fence. she also looks as if she had been crying because she has dark circles under her eyes and it looks as if her eyeliner is now smeared. she also looks as if she has alot of hate and anger in her eyes by the expression on her face. I think that im also saying this is because I know what its like to be behind a fence like that and not being able to leave. I wonder if she ever thought the way I do when shes locked up. all I can do is think of going home and rethinking of the thing I did to get in here and I think why did I do that? I was so stupid? I keep wishing why cant I just rewind the whole thing? do it all over again and I wouldn't be here? I wonder if she wishes she could do the same. just rewind it back so it wouldn't come to the point of doing what we did to get locked up. I wonder if she regrets doing what she did. because I know that I did. and I hope that I never have to go to the point of ending up where she is right now?

Sands (girl), age 16

Some of the girls' writings reflect their ability to place themselves in the shoes of the people depicted in the stories and photos they were shown. While some of the stories reflect hope, others demonstrate a sense of inevitability...

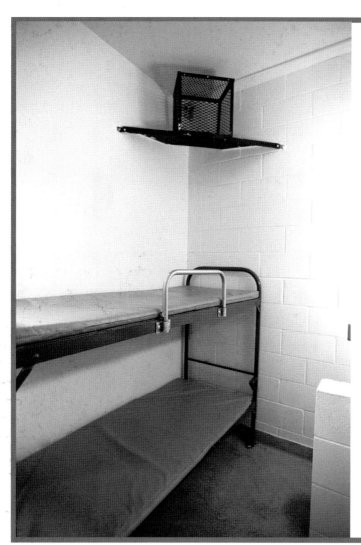

I see a clean lonely cell waiting for someone to fill it in with sadness and madness and for someone to spend sometime their or a lifetime,

And I see a room that is just alone waiting for it to be someones thinking home and rebilitation home.

I see a little block cell that now one would want to end up in.

Gonzoles (boy), age 17

You can hear the youth's conflict and ambivalence. It's both a place that "no one would want to end up in" and a "home"—a "clean" but lonely place to think and rehabilitate. For many of these youths, there is a sense of madness and sadness, a lonely void. Even a place of refuge, whether it be home or detention cell, is unspeakably isolated.

I feel . . .

I feel really bored and angry. My heart is broken and my life has fallen apart. I wonder how something can repair this wound that lys in my heart. I'm really depressed. Sitting in a room all alone. Everything inside of me is about to explode. I feel miserable. My family members abandoned me. Its hard my friend Shirley left me. And all I have is my sister. No one cares anymore. My mom doesn't come see me regularly like other people's parents. Some of my friends parent visit them every day, yet, mine barely now. I haven't heard from my dad and mom in a long time. I haven't seen my brother in a year, I haven't seen my other brother in months. Life is so depressing. My boyfriends somewhere in an unknown world. I haven't heard from him in a long time. My homies also abandoned me. I no longer have anyone except a couple of friends. I want to change this life around except how... I can't bring a brother back out from the Hall. He's been charged as an adult. Maybe 8 or 9 years until I see him again. Why is my life filled with so much misery? Is there a lesson to be taught more than I've learned? Why? Why! Is this a clue telling me that Cinderella has or is gonna meet prince charming or is the prince going to get kissed by the princess? My main concern is why? why is this happening to me? I know I've commited a crime, but this punishment is way beyond the border lines. I got sentenced to 210 days and now! It seems like I'm getting sentenced with more than the Judge gave me. My main question is why? why is it happening to me? by coincidence or do things happen there are meanings for happening? Why? Why? Why? The time I spend in here is really bad, yet why so much time. I ran a ged program, but yet I don't get anything for it. I might as well just give up a do bad. I'm a team leader, yet no one listens. They always ignore me. Are they just ignorant people? Why? Why? Why? Why? Why? Why? Why? Why? Why me!

Hui (girl), age 15

Sentiments such as "why," "why me," "everyone is ignoring me," and "I might as well be bad because I am not getting acknowledged for being good" are in many ways typical of adolescent thinking. The unfortunate part is that these youths go through a revolving door of institutions, and go from no rules at home—or chaos or unpredictable and unreasonable rules—to very rigidly enforced rules in detention. But no one is really helping them to develop critical thinking skills, to test out their ideas, or to learn cognitive skills that will allow them to problem solve and look at issues from many different vantage points. Developmentally, they become "arrested" in this adolescent thinking style. Fortunately, many probation departments are now working hard to implement evidence-based interventions that underscore the development of thinking and coping skills. But correction-based interventions alone cannot combat what life is like for these youths at home and in their neighborhoods. We need broader solutions.

(ADULT)

A puppy or dog. Sitting maybe waiting for it's owner. Maybe that person abandoned it's special animal. A lost soul could be like a puppy. Wandering, searching, waiting to be touched, loved, or carossed. Wanting a home. Waiting for security and a lil food. Loyal and abedient, trained, and in training. Like a child.

Morinski (girl), age 16

This young woman is definitely identifying with the dog and imagines the animal wanting, and waiting patiently for, comfort. The passage illustrates the youth's capacity for empathy and ability to take the perspective of another.

Although girls represent a minority of arrested and detained youths, the rate of arrest for girls is notably increasing, particularly for violent crimes. Girls comprise approximately 30 percent of arrested youths. Unfortunately, most data available on delinquents is based on studies that focus exclusively on boys. Emerging data on girls suggests higher rates of psychopathology, exposure to stress and trauma—particularly sexual trauma—and familial risk factors. It may be that, generally speaking, girls require a greater biological and/or environmental push either to engage in significantly disruptive behavior or to become officially detected delinquents.

While the essays written by girls for this project underscore issues of abandonment, substance use, and longing, they also suggest reason for hope. The insight and eloquence illustrated by these girls suggest a number of cognitive strengths and potential resiliency that could be bolstered with developmentally appropriate interventions.

This young....... well actually old woman looks as though her life has been so rough. I think you took this picture to share the pain of her face. So stern and not trusting. Scared to believe anymore. Maybe she feels like there is no hope anymore. She looks like she waits for something special or bad to happen. Struggling with emotions she wants to hide or has hidden for a long time. I think she wonders am I real. Am I a person who desires things. Am I special. "HER THOUGHTS" "Will or can I obtain these things."

Morinski (girl), age 16

The writing elegantly reflects the tension expressed by many incarcerated girls—longing to connect and be taken care of versus abandonment and difficulty trusting others due to their painful life experiences. The lives of detained youths are characteristically—although not universally—marked by high levels of stress, impoverished environments, neglect, and direct and indirect exposure to violence. This degree of micro- and macro-level instability permeates their lives, narrows their options, and serves to make them vigilant against even minor betrayals of trust. This impact is particularly palpable among incarcerated females— young and old.

Puberty

The first thing that comes to my mind when I think of puberty is growing up. I remember when I was twelve, my friends and I couldn't wait to reach thirteen, because to us, it seemed so old. Every thing really started at the teens: make-up, boyfriends, kissing (and other things), more privelages, your period (which for some reason everyone wanted until they finally got it), and curves. (Some of us, though, never get the last one.)

And that was true to me. I was always the ugly, fat duckling until my 13th. After that, over the next couple months, it changed: my face suddenly always had make-up on, the fat on my stomach disapeered and went elsewhere unto my thighs & hips (ugh.) and, my chest.

Some of the girls beautifully articulate their developmental milestones such as puberty and dating. Research conducted by Moffitt, Caspi and Obeidallah, among others, suggests that early maturing girls—those who have an earlier onset of puberty—and those who go to mixed-gender schools and/or live in disadvantaged neighborhoods are much more likely to engage in violent behavior.

Also, while research indicates that cognitive impairment, particularly in the verbal domain, is relatively common among delinquents, the girls whose thoughts are captured on these pages appear less impaired from an expressive-language perspective than their male counterparts.

And people noticed this, too. Oh, boy, did they notice; by the time the spring came, I was used to people "admiring" my assets. (Even my best guy friend once told me the reason why he loved hugging me was because I was, uh, soft and comfortable. Pig.)

It was suprising, yet flattering. I had guys asking me for my number left & right, when just the year before I couldn't even make them take the first three digits.

Puberty is a great thing; it means you're becoming a woman. The problem is, some girls take puberty as an excuse to grow up to fast.

I know some 14 year old girls who are trying to get pregnate just because their 00-something year old boyfriends are ready.

Two years ago they were playing

Pendleton (girl), age 16

with barbies, and now they think, even though they can barely take care of themselves, that they can have a baby?

And some 14-15 year olds look 5-10 years older; that doesn't mean they have the mentality or emotional stabability.

And uh, if their way older boyfriends were worth anything, they wouldn't have anything to do with a girl, and I mean girl, that young.

It destresses me how girls use puberty as an excuse to try things they arent ready for. Even though your mother might cry a tear of joy because "her baby's becoming a woman" at your first period doesn't mean her baby is a woman yet, nor does she have to act like one.

Puberty is an experience between childhood & being an adult. Don't make that mistake & grow up too fast; once your childhood's gone, you can't get it back.

Do you think after your release, you'll come back if not, what will you do to make sure you won't return? *I know I'll either come back or end up dead.*

Are you in school? If not do you have any plans to go back and finish? *No*

What have you given deep thought to since you have been in Juvenile Hall? *How not to get caught*

If you have one wish to change something in your life, what would it be? *To have a family.*

Have you ever been subjected to peer pressure? If so, how did it make you feel? How would you change it if you could and why? *It made me wanna do it.*

Do you feel your contribution can help kids stay out of trouble? If not, what needs to happen? *Start hitting your kids at a young age.*

I am a young person scared about the future. I am scared that *I might have responsibilities.*

I want *freedom*

I hope that *I get what I want.*

I feel like *I'll never make it.*

I *beat on things* when I am upset.

I wish I could be alone and find some peace and quiet. If I could then everything would be all right. Then I would *die here.*

Circle one and explain to us why.

I (like/**dislike**) school? *Too much control + responsibility*

I (like/**dislike**) my siblings. *They don't want me.*

I (like/**dislike**) family members.

I wish at times that I could live alone. (**T**/F)

I wish at times someone would understand me. That person would be *close* to me.

I feel education is *shit*.

If I could share something important with you I would tell you *Take care of your kids cause it sucks when no one cares.*

Yale (boy), age 15

This youth expresses a very common sentiment regarding what he believes his life will be like. In our research, when we ask incarcerated youth about their specific "plans" for the future, they rarely articulate anything realistic (they hope to be a rap star, a movie star, a supermodel), but when we ask them what they *think* will happen, they say they will either spend their lives in and out of jail or wind up dead.

Yale (boy), age 15

He's demonstrated a lot of conflicting ideas typical within the population: "Start hitting your kids at a young age" is juxtaposed with "Take care of your kids 'cause it sucks when no one cares."

It's unrealistic that society expect kids who have never known consistent love or care to treat animals or other people with love or respect. But these kids will go on to have children of their own, if they haven't already. The cycle perpetuates itself. We have to decide as a society that we value teaching respect for life—totally independent of religion—and implement programming early in development that teaches our youth about parenting and caring for life, in all its forms.

I see a bathroom in a jail cell. I see no freedom, no privacy, no life. I see a place of confinement, a place of punishment, a place with no happiness. I see me!

Grady (boy), age 16

Again, these youths absolutely have a pervasive and persistent visualization of their futures as bleak. One symptom of posttraumatic stress disorder is a foreshortened sense of future.

Regardless of PTSD, most kids who are locked up have already experienced a lifetime of chronic stress and exposure to trauma, even if "indirectly" (domestic-violence exposure, community-violence exposure) and/or through their own participation in gang activity. They believe that their lives will be intense, brief, and bracketed by periods of incarceration.

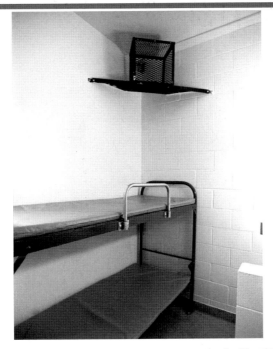

a cell. a lonely place, a place TO THInK
OF YOUR RegReTs, a place where YOUR teaRs
speak. YOUR eyes want TO see THe sun, moon, staRs.
The place where you TaLK TO GOD. YOU DiscipLine
and LeaRn youR lesson. A place wHeRe some people
DeseRve TO Be. yeT some people DONT. YOUR
sapness, youR FeaR, youR madness, insaneness,
TeaRs, come ouT. some people Have no Feeling
OR THouGHTs. spend a sHORT OR Long Time a
place weRe you Hope. I Feel I can do betteR
In LiFe, THIs isnT wHeRe I need TO Be.
I need TO FOLLOW my DReams. noT spend
my Time In HeRe. I PRay everyday In my
cell. I THInk, RememBeR, Learn, wanT, cRY,
see THIngs I DONT wanT TO see but THaT's
THe same THIng ouTsIDe OF HeRe excepT I'm
being Locked In a box wondebIng TO GOD
wHat wILL Happen. my dReam Is TO DO
someTHIng wITH PHOTOGRaPHy also. I wIll
FULLFILL THat ouTsIDe OF HeRe

Langdon (girl), age 15

Few people fully appreciate what it feels like to have your every movement controlled by someone else, including the most basic needs such as eating or access to a toilet. A cell really amplifies that lack of autonomy and sense of isolation. Despite the behavior that resulted in each youth's arrest, they are developmentally children. It is a very lonely place in which to reflect and "a place where your tears speak," says it all.

Like all aspects of juvenile justice, the issue is complicated. These youths need and even crave structure, safety, and consistency—just like any child. And they must learn to be accountable for their actions. However, our juvenile-justice system is not equipped to be the de facto mental health institution, family substitute, and special education system that is needed to address the problems that underlie many of these youths' behaviors.

Seda (boy), age 15

Violence is the primary mode of communication, the main currency for large segments of our society. If you know what goes on behind closed doors, you quickly find that communicating with violence is not at all tied to socioeconomic status or gang activity—although that may be what gets illustrated most in detention settings.

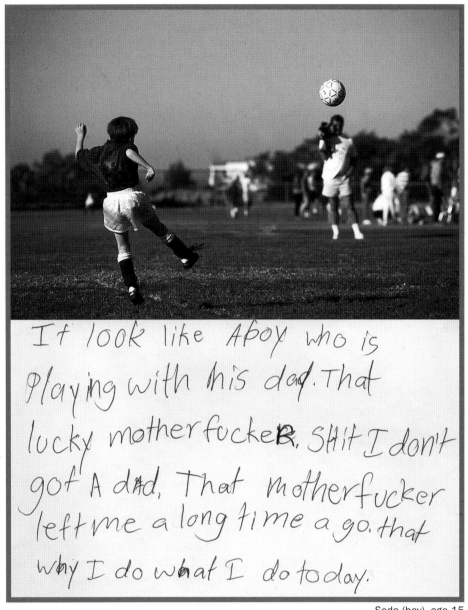

It look like Aboy who is Playing with his dad. That lucky motherfuckeR. SHit I don't got A dad, That motherfucker left me a long time a go. that why I do what I do today.

Seda (boy), age 15

Another frequent theme—many of these youths don't know their dads. At a fundamental level there is a feeling of abandonment when they are locked up, even if they are relatively close with their family.

The idea of "throwaway" lives applies to how these youths view themselves. There's a lot of anger and resentment about losing their freedom, being separated from family, being abandoned by parents (usually dads) and generally feeling as if they don't have a lot of things that others do (not just things, but family too).

Questionnaire: RC
boys night 1   **Packet Number:**

Initials:
Unit: F400
Age: 16

1) Is this your first time being in Juvenile Hall? If not, how many times have you been here? I Have Been here twice.

a) Is Juvenile Hall like you thought it would be? Why/why not?
No. I didn't think of how it would be. I wasn't expecting on comin here

b) When you get out of Juvenile Hall what would you like to accomplish for other young people so they don't have to experience Juvenile Hall?
I don't know. All I know is I'm gonna get into school at U.C. & get my licence, & a Job so I can pay my fines

2) Do you think after your release, you'll come back if not, what will you do to make sure you won't return? No. I will be gettin into school & working so I can stay out of trouble.

3) Are you in school? If not do you have any plans to go back and finish?
Yes. Hopefully After High school I can go to collage. The only way I will get there is By Playing Basketball.

4) Do you have a positive role model that you can talk to?
Yes. My mom But she can't really relate to me cause I'm A man & she's a girl

5) Do you have any family members that have been, or are in jail or prison?
My step Father is in the Pen. ~~But I think~~

6) What are your plans for the future?
Go to college after High school, And Play Basketball in the N.B.A.

7) What have you given deep thought to since you have been in Juvenile Hall?
I've given deep thought to my education. It seems now I'm more intrested in learning since I've Been in here.

8) If you have one wish to change something in your life, what would it be?
I ~~would~~ would change getting locked up For the first time. Because if I didn't get locked up that first time, I think I wouldn't Be here now.

9) Remember when you used to dream as a small child. What did you want to be when you grew up? A Basketball Player.

Taylor (boy), age 16

A lot of our kids don't know their dads because the dads are incarcerated, using drugs, etc. Their dads, even if they're not present, are still role models, even if that modeling is negative. This is a huge social problem: violence as an accepted mode of communication, and incarceration of males as a way of life. What else is there to aspire to, really? It's a miracle that anyone survives this cycle, much less gets out.

10) Have you ever been subjected to peer pressure? If so, how did it make you feel? How would you change it if you could and why?

Yes, The first time I smoked Bud.(weed) ~~It made me feel~~ It didn't make me feel anything. I would not have gave in. That way I would not be addicted to

11) What was your most memorable event (in your past)? Bud.(weed)

Nothin yet.

12) Do you feel your contribution can help kids stay out of trouble? If not, what needs to happen?

No, I Have made no contribution yet. But IF I DO It will Be to Help kids that are locked up to change Their mentality, & Hopefully they will change.

13) I am a young person scared about the future. I am scared that

I am scared that what my future holds will Be not what I want. But at the same time I think I'm the only one that can control my future.

14) I am a young adult. I can graduate from high school and I am worried about:

a) Not Beaing Abel to affosd my close.

b) Not making my mom happy.

c)

15) I want To Be ~~se~~ sucessfull at what ever I try to do in the future.

16) I hope that I can make my mom happy.

17) I feel like I need to repay my mom for all the stress.

18) I smoke Bud **when I am upset.**

19) I wish I could be alone and find some peace and quiet. If I could then everything would be all right. Then I would

20) I have 1 ~~brothers and~~ sisters.

Circle one and explain to us why.

21) I (like/dislike) school? Because it will help me in the future.

22) I (like/dislike) my siblings. She is my sister

23) I (like/dislike) family members. Exept my mom & sister

Taylor (boy), age 16

It's good that he's still reflecting some hope for himself here. The problem is that, once kids are locked up, their chances of staying out of the system are very slim, in part because of violations of probation (VOPs), the conditions of which are totally unrealistic. Seriously, how can they avoid known gang members and/or criminals who reside in their homes or neighborhoods? How many adolescents never violate a curfew? Most of these kids keep getting locked up for VOPs, not new offenses, and this is particularly true for our minority youth. It's heartbreaking that for many of these young people, their hope of—and even active attempts at—staying out of detention are nearly futile because of social policy issues and the reality of so many of our urban neighborhoods.

Long Lasting Love!

Minton (boy), age 15

People forget these are just kids, after all. Do they commit crimes? Sure. Should they be held accountable? Sure. Does our system work? Not a chance.

These are kids who simply want to know and feel love. There is a public perception that these youths are beyond redemption, have no empathy, and can't form attachments. In truth, that perception reflects only a small percentage of youths who are detained and/or incarcerated.

I am a young person scared about the future. I am scared that *I will be a loser the rest of my life*

I am a young adult. I can graduate from high school and I am worried about:
a) *my self*
b) *killing myself on the outs*
c) *getting addicted too Drugs again*

I want *lots of love*

I hope that *it will find me*

I feel like *a rat in a cage with no way out*

I _*Sleep*_____ when I am upset.

I wish I could be alone and find some peace and quiet. If I could then everything would be all right. Then I would *go nuts*

If I could share something important with you I would tell you
Why I'm fucked in the head

Oberlin (boy), age 16

Another expression of the "living hell" many of these kids experience. Delinquent youths disproportionately attempt and commit suicide. Depression is a common mental illness in this population, and internalizing symptoms—one measure of depression—is a particular red flag for potential suicidality among boys.

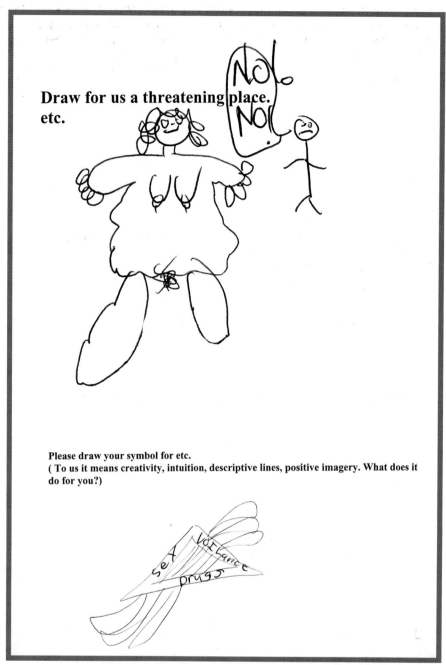

Bramble (boy), age 17

This youth's language and drawings—his exhibitionism—are clearly meant to provoke. Hyper-sexualized and provocative behavior is very common among sexually abused youths. These comments and pictures absolutely cry out for help.

Do you think man evolved from apes or do you believe in the Garden of Eden?
Defend your response with some thoughts you've had regarding how we humans got here.

we got here by fuck between
Man and woman

mean
mother and father

If you were told to create the perfect environment (place to grow up) what would it be like?
Include the following items:
1. education – girls
2. food – tweek
3. place to sleep – sex Hotel with a girl
4. clothes - style – gangsta
5. other things – girls sex

Draw for us a space you like to go for 'your time' - a time of peacefulness.

Hotel 6

most important 5 things in my is
1 my family because I love them
2. Sex because I got to have it
3. Drugs I love them too
4. more sex
5. more sex and drugs
4. my gun - because It protects me
5. beer - It get me ready to go to
work on those girls:

Bramble (boy), age 17

1) Is this your first time being in Juvenile Hall? If not, how many times have you been there? YES

a) Is Juvenile Hall like you thought it would be? Why/why not?
NO, ITS A PLACE TO THINK OF WHAT YOU DID.

b) When you get out of Juvenile Hall what would you like to accomplish for other young people so they don't have to experience Juvenile Hall?
EVERYONE HAS TO LEARN FOR THEMSELVES ESPECIALLY WHEN THEY'RE YOUNG.

2) Do you think after your release, you'll come back if not, what will you do to make sure you won't return? NO, IM GOING TO GET BACK IN SCHOOL AND NOT MAKE THE SAME MISTAKES.

3) Are you in school? If not do you have any plans to go back and finish?
NO IM NOT. YES

4) Do you have a positive role model that you can talk to?
MY. DAD

5) Do you have any family members that have been, or are in jail or prison?
MY DAD WAS IN JAIL.

6) What are your plans for the future?
GRADUATE AND RAISE MY KID.

7) What have you given deep thought to since you have been in Juvenile Hall?
MY GIRL THATS RAISING MY KID WITHOUT ME WHILE IM IN HERE

8) If you have one wish to change something in your life, what would it be?
THE DRUGS AND THE CRIMES I'VE COMMITED

9) Remember when you used to dream as a small child. What did you want to be when you grew up? I USE TO WANT TO BE JUST LIKE MY DAD,

10) Have you ever been subjected to peer pressure? If so, how did it make you feel? How would you change it if you could and why? YES, I DID DRUGS TO FEEL GOOD AND I WISH I NEVER DID.

Moore (boy), age 16

The comment that "everyone has to learn for themselves" is insightful in ways this youth probably can't imagine. The developing brain, through childhood and adolescence, is exquisitely designed for learning. We now understand that there are waves of overproduction of gray matter, followed by pruning in development. These phases occur in different functional brain areas at different points in development. We are even learning that development in the prefrontal cortex—the part that makes us so "us," so human, is responsible for planning and decision making, and plays a prominent role in social behavior and empathy—extends not only until late adolescence and the early 20s but even into the 30s and 40s.

You can't rush development, nor should you want to do so. To expect an adolescent to learn only by hearing rules is unrealistic. Trial-and-error learning is part of the human condition. Again, that doesn't mean no rules, it simply means that the developmental context is key and we, as the adults, must be smarter about how, when, and why we intervene.

11) What was your most memorable event (in your past)?

FINDING OUT THAT MY GIRL WAS PRENANT

12) Do you feel your contribution can help kids stay out of trouble? If not, what

NO, EVERYONE NEEDS TO LEARN FOR THEMSELVES.

13) I am a young person scared about the future. I am scared that

MY KID WILL END UP LIKE ME.

14) I am a young adult. I can graduate from high school and I am worried about:
a) MY GIRL
b) MY KID
c) MY SELF

15) I want TO NOT MAKE THE SAME MISTAKES

16) I hope that I LEARN FROM THIS EXPERIENCE

17) I feel like THE WORLDS AGAINST ME

18) I _HATE_ **when I am upset.**

19) I wish I could be alone and find some peace and quiet. If I could then everything would be all right. Then I would ORGANIZE MY THOUGHTS

20) I have _2_ ~~brothers~~ **and sisters.**

Circle one and explain to us why.

21) I (like/dislike) school?

22) I (like/dislike) my siblings.

23) I (like/dislike) family members.

24) I wish at times that I could live alone. (T/F)

25) I wish at times someone would understand me. That person would be _CLOSE_ **to me.**

26) I feel education is _NEEDED_ .

27) If I could share something important with you I would tell you ABOUT ME.

Moore (boy), age 16

This young man is feeling overwhelmed by his circumstances—wishing for an opportunity to organize his thoughts. He doesn't want to live alone, is thinking of his girlfriend and baby, wants to help raise the child—so from that perspective there is reason for hope. This is a youth who appears able to form attachments, thinks about others, at least wants to take responsibility.

Very few of the writings "appear" to reflect criminals—these are adolescents talking about the life they face, in all its limitations and developmentally inappropriate burdens.

13) I am a young person scared about the future. I am scared that

I wount Find a Job and be lonly and homeless wont be albible to Pay For wdat I want

14) I am a young adult. I can graduate from high school and I am worried about:

a) Job
b) life
c) Family

15) I want to be good ~~too~~ work for P.B.

16) I hope that I will live a good a better life than be for

17) I feel like Shit, becouse I'm in here but I also feel great becouse I'm clean

18) I _listen to music_ **when I am upset.** and calm down or Play the PlayStation

19) I wish I could be alone and find some peace and quiet. If I could then everything would be all right. Then I would go to my girl and go out some where or go Jump or race bikes (BMX)

20) I have _3_ **brothers and sisters.** 1 brother at home and 2 older brother somewhere else

Circle one and explain to us why.

21) I (like/~~dislike~~) school? becouse Its boring but now I will Try my best is School

22) I (~~like~~/dislike) my siblings. I used to hate my brother at home now we are ~~so~~ close rela tiotio

23) I (like/~~dislike~~) family members. becouse They all treat me with Respect

24) I wish at times that I could live alone. (T/F) becouse you can do what you want but it might get you back into

25) I wish at times someone would understand me. That person would be trouble _honest_ **to me.**

26) I feel education is _very Important_ becouse you need it to go through life

27) If I could share something important with you I would tell you I love you or Something

Wayne (boy), age 15

This youth wants someone who understands him *and* is honest with him. That is noteworthy even among high-functioning adults.

A surprising number of these kids are incredibly open and responsive to authenticity. Adolescents in general are exquisite detectors of BS, particularly from adults. They crave honesty over denial or burying their heads in the sand. They almost defy you to tell the truth and not sugarcoat things.

Questionnaire: RC
boys night 1

Packet Number:

Initials:
Unit:
Age:

1) Is this your first time being in Juvenile Hall? If not, how many times have you been there?

yes !

   a) Is Juvenile Hall like you thought it would be? Why/why not?

   no, because it is boring and strict.

   b) When you get out of Juvenile Hall what would you like to accomplish for other young people so they don't have to experience Juvenile Hall?

   I like to have after school activities, and Saturdays activities, for younger people, to keep them away from gang's.

2) Do you think after you're released you'll come back? If not, what will you do to make sure you won't return?

No, I will listen to my parents, and girl friend, and I will also look for a job.

3) Are you in school? If not do you have any plans to go back and finish?

yes !

4) Do you have a positive role model that you can talk to?

no !

5) Do you have any family members that have been, or are in jail or prison?

Yes, my Uncle, and older cousin

6) What are your plans for the future?

to have a good job, and my own apartment by the time I turn 18.

7) What have you given deep thought to since you have been in Juvenile Hall?

yes, I hope to ~~good~~ do good and work.

8) If you have one wish to change something in your life, what would it be?

not to be walking, and pay attention to my elders, and true homeboy's,

9) Remember when you used to dream as a small child. What did you want to be when you grew up?

a fireman, or a police officer.

Flanders (boy), age 15

This youth talks about listening to his parents as a way not to recidivate, yet says he has no positive role models... While this could mean that he doesn't see his parents in a positive light (a conclusion some might jump to because he does have family members who are incarcerated), it is just as possible that—from a cognitive-developmental perspective—he has not really learned what a role model is or come to understand that he can, in fact, learn from his parents.

1) **Significant people in your life:** myself

a) who brings you into Juvenile Hall? Police

b) who picks you up from Juvenile Hall? foster people

c) who do you love? myself

d) who do you respect? myself & anybody who deserves Respect

e) who do you admire? Jumier Jagr

2) **Write us what you remember about these topics and at what age.**

a) remember being scared? When I was ten I was affrail of freddy clouger

b) steal something? ever since I was eight I was on my own

c) help a friend? when my best friend got shot I took care of him until the ambulance came

d) question your happiness? havent really ever had something 2 be happy about

3) **What is a family?** dont know

4) **Has anyone ever called you stupid? If so when, and did you believe him/her?**
Yeah and no I didnt believe them

5) **Have you ever had a pet? What kind of pet and what do you remember about it?**
A rottwieler and what I Remember is He acted like a Person

6) **Is this your first time in Juvenile Hall? If not, how many times have you been in here?**
No I've been here 5 or 6 times and 2 camp once

7) **Who do you consider a role model in your life? Why?**
Nobody

8) **What was your most memorable event in your past?**
When my mom died

Bass (boy), age 15

All of these answers indicate loneliness, an isolated life devoid of happiness—no role models, stealing because he was on his own since age eight. The only person he lists as significant in his life is himself (ditto for whom he loves), and the most memorable event was the death of his mom. Yet he stayed with and took care of his friend who was shot until the ambulance arrived. Most of these kids run when there is a shooting so they don't get "caught up"—arrested, detained, taken to the police station, or sent to the children's emergency shelter.

I am a young person scared about the future. I am scared that

I wont make nothing about my life

If I could share something important with you I would tell you

always look over your back and trust no one

A Homeless Person making a friend out of a dog and treats the dog like a PeRSon

Bass (boy), age 15

Wow. "I won't make nothing about my life." "Always look over your back and trust no one."

And yet this is the same youth who commented about his dog being like a person. Despite all his incredible losses, he really does form attachments, expresses a desire to have a family, sees the life and value in animals. These are significant strengths, yet we know statistically the chance of him making it out of the system is very, very slim.

1) What do you think Universities are like? Socially and Academically?

I think their pretty cool, because you could go and learn a trade or something. Grades are like candy ~~if you them~~ ~~be~~ ~~~~ ~~~~ ~~~~ ~~~~ ~~~~ your going to keep wanthing them and wanting them. I would like to attend a University.

a) If you were to go to a large University what would be the hardest challenges to overcome?

High school and, the late nights your going to have to stay up to get good and average grades. Cramming until your brains pop out your ears. So I think thats one hell of a challenge.

b) How do you think you could help yourself to overcome the challenges that you've mentioned?

Stick to what's on ~~~~ my mind. And don't ever let nothing get in my path. Stick to my goals and dreams to be.

c) What do you think has to happen to be eligible for a University?

Have a certain grade point average. And keep sending recommedations into all the universitys. or keep buging the dean.

2) If I could share something important with you I would tell you to help me out . Please!!

Brown (boy), age 15

In contrast to young people who mostly express hopelessness, this young man demonstrates the ability to imagine himself in a different place—engaged in a very different life. That ability is a lifeline. Few incarcerated youths are actually able to visualize what it might be like to go to college ("cramming," becoming a doctor)—even when they can tell you that education is important.

While being able to "pull yourself up by your bootstraps"—to become anything you set your mind to

Write us about your thoughts.

I cant explain them that good but I would really want to be a doctor or a football player. I'd love to be a doctor because the human body sounds good to work on and you get paid money for working on them. And a football player you have so many eyes on you at all times. I would love to be the wining person to toss the wining pass.

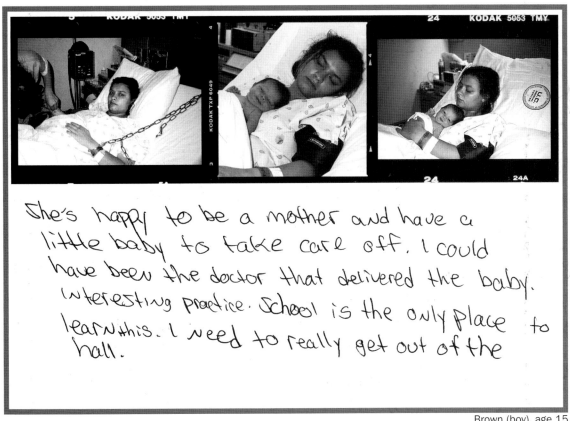

She's happy to be a mother and have a little baby to take care off. I could have been the doctor that delivered the baby. Interesting practice. School is the only place to learn this. I need to really get out of the hall.

Brown (boy), age 15

be—exemplifies the American cultural belief system, we must acknowledge that it is exceptionally difficult for these youths to rise above their circumstances and overcome their arrest history. Even though some of their juvenile records will be sealed, they are still known to the system, still known by the police in their community, and still living in circumstances that are disadvantaged, both historically and currently. It narrows their realistic prospects and it is rare to overcome these odds.

I am a young person scared about the future. I am scared that I'm not going to have a good job and be able to afford a house by myself.

I am a young adult. I can graduate from high school and I am worried about:
a) college
b) job in the future
c) How I'm going to deal with my life in the future.

I want to have a good job in the future

I hope that I won't ever come back here after I get out or go to prison.

I feel like that I'm going to have a hard time when I get out of here.

I get violent (punch) **when I am upset.**

I wish I could be alone and find some peace and quiet. If I could then everything would be all right. Then I would just try and sort out stuff with my parents

Circle one and explain to us why.

I (like/dislike) school? because I just don't like sitting there and doing boring work

I wish at times someone would understand me. That person would be a good friend **to me.**

I feel education is good .

If I could share something important with you I would tell you how your life was when you growing up,

I feel education is good .

If I could share something important with you I would tell you how your life was when you growing up,

This youth is really trying to answer these questions honestly, and he is reflecting concerns—going to college, getting a job, dealing with his life—that resonate with a wide range of people. He also demonstrates insight into his need to work through issues with his parents, and acknowledges his limitations—that he can't sit still in school, becomes violent when he is upset.

Questionnaire: RC
boys night 1

Packet Number:

Initials:
Unit: 400
Age: 15

1) Is this your first time being in Juvenile Hall? If not, how many times have you been there? a lot

a) Is Juvenile Hall like you thought it would be? Why/why not?
because I thought it would be hard.

b) When you get out of Juvenile Hall what would you like to accomplish for other young people so they don't have to experience Juvenile Hall?
Just tall them ~~to~~ don't let anyone see you

2) Do you think after your release, you'll come back if not, what will you do to make sure you won't return? I know I will come Back.

3) Are you in school? If not do you have any plans to go back and finish?
No

4) Do you have a positive role model that you can talk to?
No

5) Do you have any family members that have been, or are in jail or prison?
Yes

6) What are your plans for the future? ~~Don't know~~
I don't have plans for the future because I live life one day at a time.

7) What have you given deep thought to since you have been in Juvenile Hall?
Nothing

8) If you have one wish to change something in your life, what would it be?
nothig

9) Remember when you used to dream as a small child. What did you want to be when you grew up? a fire man

10) Have you ever been subjected to peer pressure? If so, how did it make you feel? How would you change it if you could and why? yes

11) What was your most memorable event (in your past)?
Don't know !!

Reiner (boy), age 15

Most of the youths who participated in this project demonstrate a sort of ambivalence, where they bounce back and forth between the two extremes of a kind of hopeless acceptance of their fate ("I will get locked up again") and an exaggerated sense of their future ("I'll be a professional basketball player some day"). This youth gives voice to the sentiments of many incarcerated juveniles: an eclipsed sense of possibility, a foreshortened future, and profound hopelessness. There is nothing to hope for, to wish for, or worthy of remembering either on "the outs" or on "the inside." It is difficult not to feel your heart break when you sit with a child whose life experiences—at such a young age—have left him or her utterly drained.

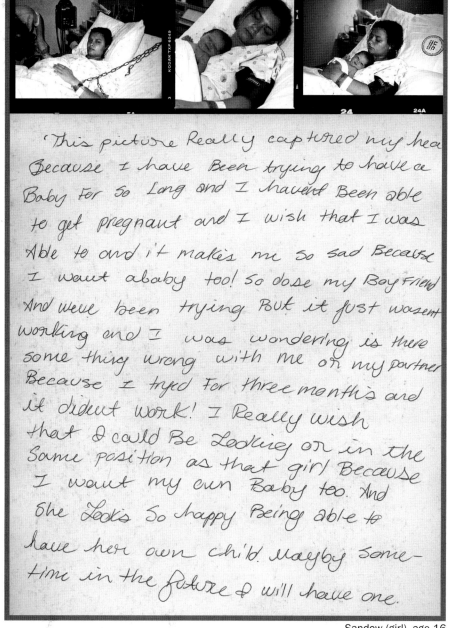

'This picture Really captured my hea
Because I have Been trying to have a
Baby For So Long and I havent Been able
to get pregnant and I wish that I was
Able to and it makes me so sad Because
I want ababy too! So dose my Boy Friend
And weve been trying But it just wasent
working and I was wondering is there
some thing wrong with me or my partner
Because I tryd For three month's and
it didnt work! I Really wish
that I could Be Looking on in the
Same position as that girl Because
I want my own Baby too. And
She Looks So happy Being able to
have her own child. Maybe some-
time in the future I will have one.

Sandow (girl), age 16

The desire to have a child is a common theme expressed by incarcerated girls. While it may be difficult for some to understand this desire, the girls simply report that they want a child whom they can love and who will love them back. Sometimes it is about proof of their love for a boyfriend and the belief that a child will prove that the person they are with also loves them. The root of this is complicated, but is related in part to attachment issues, experiences of loss, and cultural norms that transcend race and socioeconomic status. Unfortunately, these girls are ill-prepared emotionally, financially, and often physically to have a child. The fairly common desire to have a child also complicates public-policy initiatives that seek to reduce the rate of sexually transmitted diseases and improve health outcomes overall. Education about risk of disease transmission is only a partial solution to this complex issue.

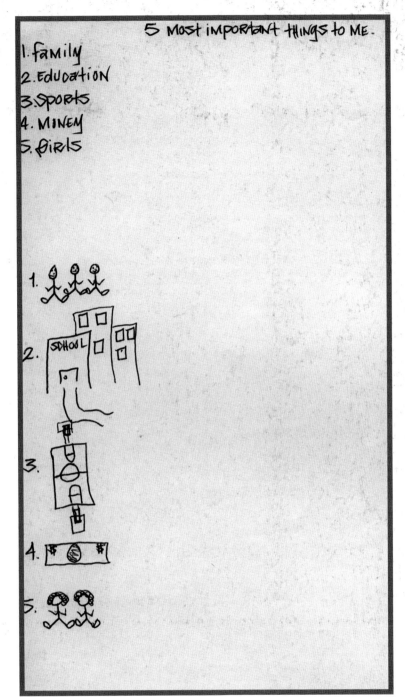

5 MOST IMPORTANT things to ME.

1. family
2. Education
3. Sports
4. MONEY
5. Girls

Armstrong (boy), age 16

Acknowledgments

I have many people to thank for their invaluable contributions to *Born, Not Raised*. First, I'm grateful to the homeless in San Diego, who shared their lives and opened my eyes to the cycles of incarceration that plague many at-risk members of society. Meeting and interviewing the homeless led to contacts within the San Diego Sheriff's Department, which led in turn to the opportunity to conduct a photojournalism project inside a local women's correction facility.

I'm grateful as well to the more than 60 women and staff I interviewed inside the jail. Many of the inmates' children were in foster care, or worse yet in detention—another cycle I wanted to explore. My work on the streets and in the jail provided the initial impetus for a project in Juvenile Hall.

Public Defender Frank Bardsley, Juvenile Hall Director Sara Vickers, Chief Deputy Randy Mize, Public Defenders Bill Boyland and Beth Shoesmith, and the many coaches all helped make the project a reality, and helped us understand the workings of the Hall and the world of juvenile justice.

I was proud and pleased when my daughter Polly chose to join me in this undertaking as credit for her psychology undergrad internship. With her professor's blessing, she worked with me throughout her internship plus an additional year beyond her graduation.

Polly is dedicated to the work of Humane Exposures. Following graduate study in graphic design, she stepped in to lend her creative talents to our many projects. Her tireless energy and commitment has not only been beneficial to the organization, it has been rewarding for me as a mother.

I wish to express my gratitude for the sensitive and brilliant efforts of Dr. Diane Campbell, who understood my passion and was willing to step in and help Polly and me process what we had experienced with these youths, many of whom were so vulnerable and unprepared for today's world. Diane spent days with us, reviewing our transcripts and listening to our unfocused thoughts—and then, finally, we got it. We could actually feel these children and the absence in their lives of what healthy and successful children take for granted—love, attachment, nurturing, and healthy curiosity.

Our growing understanding of the importance of early-childhood development led us to a conference on child abuse in Sacramento. There, we attended a lecture by Dr. Bruce Perry, Senior Fellow of the ChildTrauma Academy and an internationally recognized authority on children in crisis. Dr. Perry's insights into the neurobiological impact of trauma opened our eyes in new directions. I offer my thanks to this terrific and compassionate physician, author, and scientist, who has now contributed to two of my books and Humane Exposures' documentary film, *It's More Expensive to Do Nothing*.

Locally, Dr. Igor Koutsenok, also in our documentary film, has created and facilitated through UCSD and the DA's office a case-management program to reduce recidivism and help low-level felons get on the right track for becoming contributing members of society. Through his work, we became aware of Dr. Amy Lansing's studies in the Juvenile Hall where Polly and I had conducted our interviews and work sessions. For the first time, Polly and I were offered a scientific perspective of what we had learned and experienced with the young detainees. We have added to this book a section of Amy's professional opinions on the youths' contributions.

After 12 years of dedicated support of the work of Humane Exposures, Dr. Vincent Felitti has once again graced my book with the important Foreword. He is a remarkable physician, founder of the Department of Preventive Medicine at Kaiser Permanente, and co-author of the Adverse Childhood Experiences (ACE) Study. I am honored and grateful.

My editorial team has been working relay for the past year. When Lydia Bird—also my editor on *down-Town U.S.A.*—departed to serve as first mate on a sailing voyage to Easter Island, Anne Marie Welsh stepped in, brainstorming the project with me and working at the editing game. When Anne Marie left for India, Lydia returned to bring the ship in with me and Polly. I thank these adventurous gals.

Finally, my deep gratitude to the young people whose poignant, revealing words and artwork fill the pages of this book. One of the greatest challenges of creating *Born, Not Raised* was deciding which contributions to include and which, with regrets, to leave out. Many of the latter can be found at HumaneExposures. com. For readers who wish to look more deeply into the hopes and heartaches of our incarcerated youths.

Sources

Annie E. Casey Foundation. "The Juvenile Detention Alternatives Initiative." www.aecf.org/MajorInitiatives.aspx.

Bardsley, Frank. San Diego County Public Defender. Personal interview: March 21, 1995.

Boyland, William. Former Deputy Chief, San Diego County Public Defender. Personal interview: April 9, 1995.

Brekke, John S. et al. "How Neurocognition and Social Cognition Influence Functional Change During Community-Based Psychosocial Rehabilitation for Individuals with Schizophrenia." *Schizophrenia Bulletin* 33:5 (2007): 1247–1256.

Brekke, John S., Brandon Kohrt, and Michael F. Green. "Neuropsychological Functioning as a Moderator of the Relationship Between Psychosocial Functioning and the Subjective Experience of Self and Life in Schizophrenia." *Schizophrenia Bulletin* 27:4 (2001): 697–708.

Campbell, Diane, M.D. Personal interviews: March 2002–September 2010.

Children's Initiative. "2009 San Diego County Report Card on Children and Families." www.thechildrensinitiative.org/.

Cocozza, Joseph J. and Kathleen Skowyra. "Youth with Mental Health Disorders: Issues and Emerging Responses." *Juvenile Justice* 7:1 (2000): 3–13.

Court Cases: *Bowring v. Godwin,* 551 F. 2d 44 (4th Cir. 1977); *Estelle v. Gamble,* 429 U.S. 97 (1976); *Ruiz v. Estelle,* 503 F. Supp. 1265 (S.D. Tex. 1980); *Madrid v. Gomez,* 889 F. Supp. 1146 (N.D. Cal. 1995).

Crogan, Alan. Former Chief, San Diego County Department of Probation. Personal interview: March 25, 1995.

Donnellan, M. Brent, Xiaojia Ge, and Ernst Wenk. "Cognitive Abilities in Adolescent-Limited and Life-Course-Persistent Criminal Offenders." *Journal of Abnormal Psychology* 109:3 (2000): 396–402.

Dumanis, Bonnie. San Diego County District Attorney. Personal interview: December 4, 2009.

Felitti, Vincent, M.D. Personal interviews: July 14, 2009 and August 3, 2009.

Friedman, Howard S. and Miriam W. Schustack. *Personality: Classic Theories and Modern Research.* 4th edition. Boston: Allyn & Bacon, 2008.

Hallowell, Edward M. Shine: *Using Brain Science to Get the Best From Your People.* Boston: Harvard Business Press, 2011.

Heckman, James R. "The Heckman Equation." www.heckmanequation.org.

Jaeger, J. et al. "Neurocognitive Test Performance Predicts Functional Recovery from Acute Exacerbation Leading to Hospitalization in Bipolar Disorder." *Bipolar Disorders* 9:1–2 (2007): 93–102.

Jaeger, J. et al. "Remediation of Neuropsychological Deficits in Psychiatric Populations: Rationale and Methodological Considerations." *Psychopharmacology Bulletin* 28:4 (1992): 367–90.

Jaeger, J. et al. "Neurocognitive Deficits and Disability in Major Depressive Disorder." *Psychiatry Research* 145:1 (2006): 39–48.

Jenkins, Mack. San Diego County Chief Probation Officer. Personal interviews: July 15, 2009 and June 14, 2010.

Kelly, Joan B. and Janet R. Johnston. "The Alienated Child: A Reformulation of Parental Alienation Syndrome." *Family Court Review* 39:3 (2001): 249–266.

Klepin, Yvette. San Diego Deputy Chief of Probation. Personal interview: September 16, 2010.

Koutsenok, Igor, M.D. Personal interviews: July 15, 2009, September 21, 2009, and January 24, 2011.

Lansing, Amy. Neuropsychologist. Personal interviews and conference calls: October 2010–February 2011.

Lewis, Thomas, M.D., Fari Amini, M.D., and Richard Lannon, M.D. *A General Theory of Love.* New York: Vintage Books, 2001.

Milliken, James R. Former Chief Presiding Judge, San Diego Juvenile Court. Personal interview: July 14, 2009.

Moffitt, T.E. and D. Lynam. "The Neuropsychology of Conduct Disorder and Delinquency: Implications for Understanding Antisocial Behavior." In *Progress in Experimental Personality and Psychopathology Research,* edited by D.C Fowles, P. Sutker, and S.H. Goodman, 233–262. New York: Springer, 1994.

Perry, Bruce D., M.D. Personal interview: July 24, 2009.

Perry, Bruce D., M.D. "Traumatized Children: How Childhood Trauma Influences Brain Development." *The Journal of the California Alliance for the Mentally Ill* 11:1 (2000), 48–51.

Perry, Bruce D., M.D. "Bonding and Attachment In Maltreated Children." Adapted in part from *Maltreated Children: Experience, Brain Development and the Next Generation.* New York: W. W. Norton & Company, in preparation.

Pietrzak, Janet, Geraldine Downey, and Ozlem Ayduk. "Rejection Sensitivity as an Interpersonal Vulnerability." In *Interpersonal Cognition,* edited by Mark W. Baldwin, 62–84. New York: Guilford Press, 2005.

Raine, Adrian et al. "Neurocognitive Impairments in Boys on the Life-Course Persistent Antisocial Path." *Journal of Abnormal Psychology* 114:1 (2005): 38–49.

Saigh, Philip A. et al. "Child-Adolescent Posttraumatic Stress Disorder: Prevalence, Risk Factors, and Comorbidity." In *Posttraumatic Stress Disorder: A Comprehensive Text,* edited by Philip A. Saigh and J. Douglas Bremner, 18–43. Boston: Allyn & Bacon, 1998.

Saltzman, William R. et al. "Trauma- and Grief-Focused Intervention for Adolescents Exposed to Community Violence: Results of School-Based Screening and Group Treatment Protocol." *Group Dynamics* 5:4 (2001): 291–303.

Shankman, Henry. Probation Officer, Oceanside, California. Personal interview: August 29, 1995.

Shoesmith, Beth. San Diego County Public Defender. Personal interview: April 24, 1995.

Simmons, Charlene Wear and Emily Danker-Feldman. "Parental Incarceration, Termination of Parental Rights, and Adoption: A Case Study of the Intersection Between the Child Welfare and Criminal Justice Systems." *Justice Policy Journal* 7:2 (2010).

Swerdlow-Freed, Daniel H. "New Research on Alienated Children" (2001). www.drswerdlow-freed.com/forensicarticle4.html.

Teplin, Linda A. et al. "Psychiatric Disorders in Youth in Juvenile Detention." *Archives of General Psychiatry* 59:12 (2002): 1133–1143.

van der Kolk, Bessel A. "The Compulsion to Repeat the Trauma: Reenactment, Revictimization, and Masochism." *Psychiatric Clinics of North America* 12:2 (1989): 389–411.

Wasserman, Gail A. et al. "The Voice DISC-IV with Incarcerated Male Youths: Prevalence of Disorder." *Journal of the American Academy of Child and Adolescent Psychiatry* 41:3 (2002): 314–321.

Index

Mary, 135, 137–138
Yvette, 27
cognitive skills, 165, 168
comfort food, 123
community violence, 172
compassion, 28, 118, 153, 156
confidentiality, 41, 137
connection to others, 105, 135, 153, 160
Connolly, 24, 27
conscience, 55, 67, 74–75, 116
consistency, 47, 84, 86, 117, 171, 173
control issues, 43, 61, 71, 94, 98, 132, 173
cooperativeness at play, 75
correction-based interventions, 165
Corrections, Department of, 9
crack, 56, 61, 63
Creighton, 131f
critical thinking, 165
Crogan, Al, 3
curfew, 177
curiosity, 67, 74, 112, 116

DeCarava, Roy, 17
decision making, 42, 47, 144, 156, 182
delinquency system, 5, 10
delinquent youths, defined, 5
Department of Corrections, 9
Department of Juvenile Justice, 31, 151
Department of Probation, 3
Department of Social Services, 9
dependency court, 5
dependent youths, defined, 5
depression, 50, 52, 94, 101, 118, 130, 138, 179
derailments, 49
detention, defined, 9
development, stages of, 49–60
developmental arrest, 70, 90, 165
"divide and conquer," 86
domestic violence, 13, 58, 74, 85–86, 89–90, 109–114, 160, 172, 176
Donaldson, 91f
Donna, coach at GRF, 27–28
Downey, Geraldine, 144
drug abuse
    anger and, 61–66
    Bardsley on, 4
    Boyland on, 10
    Campbell on, 94
    Coach Kristen on, 18
    crack, 56, 61, 63
    hitting bottom and, 105
    mental illness and, 99–101
    neglect and, 144, 156
    parental, 105, 156
    Pendleton on, 84–85
    thought organization and, 183
Dubois, Amber, 110

East Mesa Juvenile Detention Facility, 140f
eating disorders, 123
education. See also learning
    about STDs, 192
    Boyland on, 10
    Campbell on, 94
    Chim on, 128
    importance of, 151
    parenting, 151
    Pendleton on, 84
    prenatal, 151

sexual aggression and, 111–112
    visualizing, 188
"eight percenters," 148
Ella Baker Center, 152
emotional abandonment, 90, 94
emotional neglect, 41, 45
empathy
    ability to love and, 144
    aggression and, 132
    anger and, 132
    for animals, 153, 166, 171, 187
    maturity and, 55
    nature vs. nurture and, 158
    nurturing and, 156
    prefrontal cortex development and, 182
    public perception of, 47, 178
    self-preoccupation and, 116
evidence-based programs and interventions, 153, 165
executive functioning, 42, 117

familial risk factors, 159, 166
families. See also parents
    affection and, 128
    Campbell on, 94
    gangs as surrogate, 34, 90–91, 150
    pseudo in GRF, 41
fantasy life, 75
Fast ForWord, 153
fathers. See also parents
    absentee, 63, 175–176
    impulse control and, 149
    Minton on, 34–35
    as role models, 176
fear
    of attachment, 138
    brain development and, 89
    Campbell on, 67
    of death, 160
    at Juvenile Court, 137
    of making mistakes, 43, 74
    of not being good enough, 43
feelings. See also impulse control; specific feelings
    fear of, 111, 138
    of importance, 43
    of inferiority, 43
    sexualized aggression and, 109–114
Felitti, Vincent, 108
Feshback, Seymour, 132
first memories, 71–73f, 74, 91
Flanders, 185f
food hoarding, 47
foster care, 3, 5, 52, 93–94, 118, 128
Freud, Sigmund, 42
Friedman, Howard S., 43
functional impairment, 161
funding issues, 9–10, 70, 144, 151
future, sense of, 156, 170, 172, 191

gang-related homicide, 4
gangs
    Bardsley on, 4
    Chim on, 34
    Coach Julie on, 132
    Coach Maria on, 37
    Morinski on, 18
    PTSD and, 172
    reasons for joining, 102
    as surrogate families, 34, 90–91, 150
gardening, 153

Shankman, Henry, 3
  Vickers on, 13–14

If all you see is hoods and hoodlums and proof of their crimes, you might not choose to undergo the trauma of this work, and it might be difficult to treat them as children.

But they're kids!

—Sara Vickers
Former Director, Kearny Mesa Detention Facility